IT WASN'T LOVE

by

JS Lee

To Gemma —
May your journey be
cathartic and rewarding.
x♡x
JS Lee

This book is dedicated to the survivors—
the brave, and the ones who still suffer in silence.
May you all find peace and empowerment
and may your journeys lead you
to love, at last.

I would like to thank the following people
for their generous support and encouragement:

Anonymous
Bruce Kohl
Debbi Wagner-Johnson
Hugh Wyman
John Robinson
Kat Park

SPRING 1992 //
ONE YEAR POST-INCIDENT

I found the guy I'm going to give my virginity to—last night in the McDonald's parking lot. We were cruising around the neighboring towns for lack of anything better to do. When we pulled in to the lot, his car full of boys screeched in after us.

We stood outside, leaning up against cars, checking each other out. Samantha was flirting with him, but he gave me his number on the sly. I caught his eye as he went in to use the restroom. On his way out, he snuck the folded up paper into my hand. I felt a spark when we made the exchange.

We talked earlier today and somehow it came up on the phone—*The Incident* and shit. I didn't go into detail or any-thing—just said that it happened. I told him I wanted to lose my virginity for real. He said maybe he could help.

I don't want to talk about *The Incident* itself. It's just

that I refuse to let it count. I'm still at zero. Nobody gets to take number one from me.

Things have been all kinds of fucked up since it happened. I'm an outsider at home and at school. It's like I'm buried ten layers deep in this cave of a girl. And for the first time it's not just because of being the only one with slanty eyes. It's this secret that's not really a secret so much as the thing we pretend not to talk about. But I hear the whispers. I hear all the subtle, not quite accusations that question everything but what needs to be questioned.

At night it's the worst. Everywhere I turn there's another projection jumping out from nowhere, catching me off guard. And the eyes—the evil, the scornful, and the disapproving eyes—I just want to close them all.

Sometimes in the middle of class I imagine my clothes tearing. An ugly rash starts bubbling out of my skin, and kids look on in horror at the shriveled up monster I've become. They look at me like it's all my fault—as if I wanted to be this monster.

Luke doesn't think I'm a monster. He doesn't know anything about me. He's so chill. He listens when I talk and doesn't try to impress. He asks questions without being a dick. It's hard to explain, but I just know that he's perfect for this.

The idea popped into my head one night when I was gazing out the window as I do. I decided that I need to do this with intention and I need it to be my idea. Maybe it'll make me feel more like a normal girl than the ghost of who I was supposed to be.

I've spent my whole life trying to please everybody and somehow it all led to this. Nothing's sacred. Nothing's worth saving for, and there's absolutely nothing that can't be stolen.

So, this thing, I'm doing for me.

PUNCHING FOOLS

My parents are still spying on my diary and it's so pathetic. Of course I put a string across it in such a way that I'd know if anyone had moved it. And what's worse is my dad is stupid enough to tell me that he likes what I wrote— *which I'd written as bait*.

"That was beautiful, what you wrote in that book," he says, as I'm matching his socks in dim light. His socks— they all look the same but with annoying subtleties. So I just nod my head and keep my face down, rolling more socks on the bed.

I'd written about how great God is and how he brought me to my family. It was bullshit, but I wanted them off my back. I don't believe in God, but my dad once contemplated priesthood. I knew that would help do the trick but didn't think he'd slip up, admitting to spying.

Dad's shaving in the bathroom adjoined to their bed-room, getting ready to go out to dinner. They go out to dinner nearly every night to get some peace and quiet, they say. He slaps on a little too much Old Spice and says nothing more of it.

It's so sad when you outsmart your parents, who keep insisting they know so much more than you do. I knew then that the balance might have shifted. He and Mom may now be more innocent than me.

And ever since I broke down in the principal's office, most of my teachers have gone easy on me. I'm a troubled girl to be given a break. So I skip more classes to drive around town, fixated on when it will happen with Luke.

"I think I figured out when we can do it," Luke says, calmly, on the phone.

I sit on the blue and white bathroom tiles with the dirty white phone cord wrapped around my arm. Don't ask why we have a phone in the bathroom—or intercoms and sur- veillance cameras in every room, for that matter.

The bathroom is one of the only rooms with a lock, and this call seems to warrant one somehow. So I sit on the floor clutching the phone, hoping no one picks up another line.

"Oh yeah?" I say to Luke, while my eyes trace the swirls of the blue and gold wallpaper.

"Yeah," he says. "I have the keys and alarm code to one of the offices I clean. We can go in anytime they're not there."

"Cool," I say, somewhat unaffected.

"So you want me to pick you up around eight on Tues- day?" he asks.

"Okay," I say.

Luke picks me up in his old-man sedan that's pimped

out with tinted windows. I walk slowly, and with a false display of security, across the long walkway in front of the house. I know he's watching with anticipation from the driveway. And I know I look cute. I made sure of it.

He gets out of the long black car to open the door for me. Inside it smells of soft vanilla on raspberry velvet upholstery. His car is impeccable. He takes care of his things, and I immediately like that.

He's more sophisticated than other guys our age. At seventeen, most guys act crass to make sure you don't think that they care. I smile to myself at how well I chose.

"How ya doin'?" he asks, with a slight smile at my appearance and maybe a twinge of nervousness.

"I'm okay," I half-smile back.

"If you want to turn around anytime, just say the words," he says, looking me in the eye for an uncomfortable moment.

"No, I'm alright," I say, looking straight ahead. But when his eyes are back on the road, I study him out of the corner of my eye.

His lashes are long and dark and highlight his pale blue eyes with their contrast. His hair and clothes are casual perfection. They fit well—not baggy and shapeless like the clothes worn by other boys in my school. And I like the way he sits calmly without needing to displace energy.

When we pull up to the office park, I wait in the car as he heads in to make sure everything's all set. He returns, opens my door, and retrieves a few things from the trunk.

I shouldn't trust a stranger for this or anything less. I know that. I've experienced what happens when you trust the wrong people. And maybe that's why I need this. For one, I can't imagine anything worse happening to me at this point. And even if I'm murdered, it may be a relief to myself and secretly to many.

So I follow Luke into the office as he lays out a blanket and some pillows in a corner of a conference room. He turns on a camping lantern.

"You sure you want to do this?" he asks, gently.

I nod, keeping quiet. There's no need for words.

Luke takes the lead by stepping forward and kissing me. His tongue moves at a nice slow pace, which takes the blow off how weird it is to be kissing a near stranger. He pats my hair all the way down my back and works his way toward undressing me.

I've always played the brave girl. Even during *The Incident*. I have pride sewn into my genes much tighter than plausible. I pretend to be into it but I'm just acting, really. Like everything I've done since that day, I go through the motions, waiting for something to make me feel real.

Luke slides a condom on above me. I start to tense.

"You okay?" he asks.

"Yep," I say, a little too nervously.

"I'll go slow," he says, softly.

But as soon as he tries, it feels like a thick pin stabbing me blind.

"Stop," I yelp, as the pressure of his body hits me on the head. He eases up. I try to undizzy myself. I take a few breaths and exhale, "Okay, try again."

This happens repeatedly for a span of time I can't possibly count.

"I don't think this is gonna work," he says, finally.

I'm so disappointed in myself. This is what I want.

"Try again. Just once more," I say. "I'll try to relax," I plead, breathing in the faint smell of his cologne, which thankfully smells nothing like Old Spice.

"Okay," he says, and slowly he starts again.

"Stop," I gasp, unsure of why my body won't cooperate. I bite my lower lip.

"Maybe you're not ready yet," says Luke. "Let's put our clothes back on," he whispers.

I wasn't ready before either, I brood to myself.

Quietly, we both move into the dimly lit office to re-dress. I'm filled with such shame. It's kind of weird, I guess, but it is what it is.

"It's okay," Luke says, reading my mind. "It doesn't always happen on the first try for everyone," he assures me.

I keep my eyes off him as I dress.

"We'll try again another time," he says, but I'm not sure I believe it.

I lie awake in bed as usual but instead of feeling angry at the world, I'm angry with myself. I punch at my psyche until I fall asleep.

RUDE AWAKENINGS

Sometimes I kind of feel like *The Incident* mentally shot me up two feet taller than everyone else.

When I unblur my ears for a moment or two during class, I want to stand up and yell, *You guys are so stupid! Everything you're saying is ridiculous and proof that you're clueless about real life! Stop whining and wake the fuck up!*

But of course, I don't.

Deep down a part of me is jealous of them and their petty normalcy. So on the surface of my conscience, I feel it's okay to belittle them. Like it or not, I know life, raw and uncensored. I know things that they've only read flowery versions of, which allude to depths without taking them there. I have perspective and they've got 2D.

Sure, they've got boyfriends to hold hands with down hallways. They've got cute little gifts from each other that are really paid for by their rich parents who spoil them rotten. And they've got so much shelter that they think a light drizzle is a storm.

I like being wizened—it's the one good thing I've gotten from this shit. The knowledge that I know more, that I know of some truths that most might never know; it's something.

I imagine a day when I might do something with these truths I've collected. I don't know. Maybe something that declares: Millie 1, Rapist 0.

I've been talking to Luke on the phone just about every night. He says if I get to know him better it might be easier—psychosomatic bullshit or something. Everything I know about him already makes him so much better than most. I'm not sure that's the problem, but I talk to him anyway.

Luke works two jobs outside of high school to help his mom pay the bills. I guess his dad didn't leave much money when he died about a year and a half ago. He cleans offices a couple nights a week and is an apprentice for an electrician. He says he's not super close with his mom or his sister, but he does what he can to help them both out.

I tell him a little about my crazy family and how I'm the only one adopted. Everyone always thinks it's so weird that I was adopted in the middle of a big white family. And I usually get jokes about my parents being nympho Catholics who don't believe in birth control. Luke doesn't say anything stupid like that, thankfully.

"What do you like to do?" he asks.

That question has never been difficult until now. "I don't know. Before. . ." I begin and switch gears. "Nothing, really. I stay up late watching movies on cable that would kill my parents if they knew I watched."

He doesn't ask about 'before' or 'before what' and I like him for that.

"What kinds of movies do you watch?" he asks.

"I don't know," I hesitate. "Soft porn," I giggle, "creepy thrillers. Pretty much everything I wouldn't want my daughter to watch."

"Do you want kids someday?" he asks.

"No!" I scoff, quickly. "No way. Never did. It's just not in me to want kids."

I pause for a moment and then ask, regretfully, "Why? Do you want kids?"

"Sure, someday," Luke says. "Not for a long time, though."

It's funny that we even have this conversation because it's never been established that we're boyfriend and girlfriend. We don't flirt. We don't do boyfriend-y, girlfriend-y things. I just want to have sex with him, and Luke is nice enough to try to make that happen for me. It's all I'm available for.

The second time we make plans, we go back to the same office, similarly equipped. Luke brings a little stereo this time. He says we can listen to anything I want. I put on some Top 40 station, not really caring what's on in the background. I'm just focused on making sure it happens this time.

We're sitting down on the blanket when he touches me. I'm too conscious of the little roll between my hips and my bra so I jump instinctively.

"What's the matter?" he asks.

"I don't like being touched there," I say.

"Why? Because your stomach folds over when you sit?

Everyone's does," he says, kissing me.

But I've always been too self-conscious. I hate the way I look. I always have.

"I think you look great," Luke says. "You have a great body."

"Let's not talk about my body," I mumble, thinking about how weird the word 'body' sounds at the moment.

"Okay then," he says, finding his way around my clothes.

When we're naked again and he's all condomed up, we try for Round Two. Luke has brought some sort of lubricant that he asks to massage onto me. I nod my head and sit awkwardly as he does so. I jump from the gooey, cold sensation.

Still my body resists him. It's as if the strength from all areas of my body forms an alliance between my legs to fend him off. My brain yells, *He's not the perp! Back off!* But the muscles are sticking together like a guard dog protecting what's left of my virginity.

"It's okay," Luke says.

"Why are you so patient?" I snap.

"Well, what's the rush?" he asks. "I'm in no hurry."

"Well, I am," I snap again and then sigh while my face starts to burn.

"You are?" he asks. "How come?"

But I don't know, so I just leave his questions hanging out there between us as we dress.

Later at night, I wonder, *Why am I in such a rush?* And for a moment, just a speck of an answer flies by. That nagging, whiny voice in my head taunts me.

Before it happens again, it says. I swat it away.

THE GREAT
BARRIER OF GRIEF

"How old were you when you first did it?" I ask Luke over the phone.

"Fourteen," he says easily.

"Fourteen?" I echo. "That's so young!"

"It was one of my sister's friends. She's a couple years older than me. They were all drunk, hanging out in the living room. She snuck into my room, took me by surprise," he says.

"Was it good?" I ask.

"Well, it was fast," he laughs. "But I was pretty excited about it. It just happened so quickly. I didn't have much time to think or enjoy the actual sex."

"How many times did you do it with her?" I ask, curiously.

"That was it. Just one time," he says.

"So how many people have you done it with?" I ask, try-ing not to sound interrogative.

"Three," he says. "That girl, a friend's sister a few months later, and then the girlfriend I had after that. We kind of did it a lot."

"Why'd you break up?" I wonder.

"After my dad died I didn't really have much time for her. I don't know. She didn't really get it. I think her friends gave her shit for putting up with me not being there or something. It doesn't really matter."

I'm not sure why, but I start to feel a little something for Luke. I guess all this talking is bringing us closer after all. He becomes more human to me.

"How did your father die?" I ask, almost wishing I hadn't as soon as the words leave my mouth.

"He was a construction worker. He fell from the scaf-folds. He wasn't in the union or anything. Just lost one job and took another short-term to keep money coming in," he says.

"I'm so sorry," I say instinctively.

"It's okay," he says in his usual calm way. "I mean—it sucks, but what can ya do?"

"I know what you mean," I say, chewing on my left cheek.

In school the next day I think about Luke as I stare out the window. It occurs to me that maybe I'm drawn to him because what happened with his dad shot him up a couple feet taller than the other kids, too. Like me, he knows life in a way that most other kids don't have to. He knows pain—*real* pain. We must've sensed it off each other.

And then I wonder if, like me, he never cries.

The third time we attempt what I've been calling in my head *The Great Barrier of Grief*, it's in Luke's house. He's got a finished basement turned into a den with a TV and pool table. It's very seventies, wood paneling and all, but pretty cool.

"What if your mother or sister comes home?" I ask nervously.

"My mom's at work and my sister's at college," he says. "There's no way anyone's coming home."

"Okay," I say, taking in my surroundings.

"Come sit on the couch," he says, taking my hand.

I follow him, feeling surprisingly at ease. He has such a comfortable presence. He's like nobody else that I know. There's an acknowledgement that I couldn't possibly have found better than this. But still, I don't feel anything strong for him. No psycho-pull the way I've felt about other less-deserving guys who never gave me the time of day.

"Tell me what you'd like me to do," he says, smiling.

"I don't know," I trail off shyly.

"Think about it," he says. "I'm sure you've got ideas about the way you'd like it to go."

I look into my head but come up empty. "I don't think I ever thought up a scenario for it," I say, twisting my mouth sideways. "I mean—I've never visualized it. I just know that I want it to happen."

"You've never visualized it? Ever?" he asks incredulously.

"Not really," I say, embarrassed.

"What do you think about when you masturbate?" Luke asks, and I turn red.

"I don't really masturbate," I say. "I mean, I used to a lot when I was young, but I didn't really get it. I wasn't sexual for other people. I just kind of explored the way it felt. But I haven't really done it in a while."

"Okay," he says, not pushing it. "Do you want me to tell you what I think about?"

"Other girls?" I say, quickly, like a moron.

"Sometimes," he says. "But mostly you."

My eyes swoop up to his, modestly.

"Don't look so surprised," he says, grinning. "Do you think I'm only doing this for you? I'm happy to help it happen your way. But I'm doing it for my own pleasure, too."

I think about what he says. *Of course he's doing it for himself*. But I guess a big part of me wanted to imagine he was just helping a girl in need. I want to be the one who wants it more.

"Okay, so what do you think about with me?" I ask shyly.

"I think about you in your pretty outfits, the way you put yourself together and smile at me," he says. "You're just different from most girls I know."

"Oh yeah?" I say, feeling flattered but wondering if by 'different' he means Asian.

"I picture you walking toward the car when I come to pick you up. It's always nice to see the door swing open and you heading my way looking the way you do."

"Thanks," I whisper awkwardly.

Luke reaches over to kiss me, and we make out a little longer than usual. He uses his hands to stroke my hair and my body, making sure that he doesn't mess me all up. I like the time he takes with me, the smell of his fresh breath, and his full attention.

Naked with a condom, he's on top of me again and I'm feeling like it's going to happen. It's more comfortable in his house than in some strange office. Being in his home creates another level of trust somehow. I run my fingers through his short, wavy, dark hair as he carefully maneuvers above me.

"Stop!" I gasp, closing up shop once again. "I'm sorry," I add.

"Just take it easy," he says. "Don't apologize."

He kisses me on the lips again, moving slowly with care. He caresses my thighs and breasts, and I try to give myself to him. But it just doesn't happen.

I sit up. "I don't know why I can't do it," I sulk, embarrassed, with my head in my hands. "It's not you. It's like my body's instinctively shutting down every time."

Luke sits alongside me as patiently as ever. "Is there anything I can do for you?" he asks.

"I don't know. Like what?" I ask.

And then he slides down off the couch and kisses my thighs as I wriggle around embarrassingly.

"What are you doing?" I exclaim. "You're tickling me!"

But after a while it stops tickling so much. I'm nearly popping his head off with my post-gymnastics thighs, but I'm not having the worst time of my life.

"Let's try it again," he says, rising up.

But still, *The Great Barrier of Grief* holds strong.

SOWING SEEDS

I don't even know what's going on in school anymore with the kids or the classes. A part of me thinks that instead of going easy on me they should've given me a year or two off. I don't know how I'll ever catch up. But then, what would I do if I were at home? I'd probably want to shoot myself.

My youngest brother is just a couple years old. He was born half a year before it happened. He's a good baby, but the house is always in chaos. Someone's always yelling about something.

My oldest sister's anorexic and nearly dying every other week or freaking us out with her nerves. There are twenty years between the youngest and oldest. And they've all got fire in their Italian blood. Well, most of them do, anyway.

The anorexic sister is going through this phase where she repeats everything you say as if it were an insulting accusation. Her presence makes me nervous. I never know if what I say will set her off.

Last night I walked into the kitchen to empty the dishwasher, but she was standing next to it already. Steam was rolling out the top of it, as it was cracked open. She looked creepy as it swirled around her sunken-in face like smoke.

I say, "Are you going to do the dishes," innocently enough, I think.

But she yells at the top of her lungs, "WHAT, MILLIE? AM I GOING TO DO THE DISHES?"

I open my eyes really wide, inhale, and just back my way out.

So all of our names begin with the letter M. It's just another family oddity. When people learn my name's Millie they immediately say, *Milli Vanilli?* As if I'd never heard it before. They laugh harder when they learn my last name's Vaniti.

Yep. My name is Millie Vaniti. You'd think if there was a God, he could've stopped at that, right? And it figures Milli Vanilli got busted for being imposters. Makes me wonder when I'm gonna get busted.

Some of my teachers look at me so sadly, and I know a couple of them hate me. My geometry teacher looks at me as if he just ate a Sour Patch Kid. I wonder if they all know about *The Incident*, and if they do, what scenarios they've painted in their heads about it—about me.

I'm tuned out again in class, lost in the shadows of my mind, when my name is called to answer a question. I couldn't even tell you which subject I'm in, I'm that far removed. I look up, snap halfway back to reality, and say, "What? Can you repeat the question?"

The kids laugh. One boy says loudly, "There you go, Millie, living up to your Asian stereotypes," for more laughter.

I know, I know. I'm supposed to be the smartest kid in class. My eyes are sharp, so my brain should be sharper. I give him the finger when the teacher turns her back. It's a way to let him think we're cool.

At home, I'm still planting seeds in the red floral diary that they spy on. Every day or two I write another passage that a perfect daughter would write. Something about God or family always works. They haven't been snooping as much, so it's working. The small string is moved less and less each week. I've actually been using two strings just to be sure they haven't caught on. It's harder to remember the exact placement of two strings. Lucky for me, my memory's nearly photographic for what's generally useless shit.

When Luke calls, I'm always so relieved to have him as my one slice of normalcy in life. I suppose the idea of scheming with my non-boyfriend about taking my non-virginity doesn't sound very normal. But to me, at this point, it's what I've got.

"My mom's on the night shift again," he says. "Want to try again here in a couple days? I'm off on Thursday."

"Yeah, that sounds good," I tell him.

"I'll pick you up around seven?" he says.

"Sure," I say.

"So what have you been doing?" he asks, now that business is out of the way.

"Nothing really," I say. "I don't know. The usual. Hiding from the loudest family in the history of human beings. Cleaning up dog shit in the backyard."

Luke laughs. "They don't get your brothers to do the dirty work?" he asks.

"Are you kidding? My brothers don't do shit." I laugh hysterically at the unintended pun. It takes me a solid minute to catch my breath. God, I'm such a loser.

"I mean, really," I say, calming down. "They get away with doing absolutely nothing. I'm always given the chores because they know I'll do 'em. Besides, I like the dogs. It's really gross for them to be out in the sun with their own poop melting ripe all around them. And sometimes they eat it."

"Uck," groans Luke.

"No joke," I say.

"Well, wash your hands before I pick you up in a couple days," he smirks. I can hear it through the phone.

"We'll see," I tease. I'm struck by how filthy the convo has turned. "I don't want to sweet-talk you all night, so see you on Thursday."

"Later," Luke says coolly before hanging up.

I wear black shorts with a thick belt and a white sleeveless blouse with ruffles down the front that tie at the bottom. I pull my hair up from the sides into a clip and let the rest of it fall down my back. I slide on hot pink lipstick and black eyeliner and strap on platform wedge sandals.

The walk from my front door to Luke's car always feels like a runway. He gets out of the car to watch me as I swing my hips slowly toward him. I glide down the three steps and pass the weird stone donkey and cart that's parked on the lower front lawn. I swing my legs into the car, looking up to admiring blue eyes before he shuts the door gently.

He listens to classic rock, but it's never loud enough to mask the awkward silence.

"You look nice." He smiles and leans across for a kiss.

"Thank you," I smile, happy to please. "You look nice, too," I add.

And he does. I'm still amazed that my heart doesn't pound for him. I think to myself, *Maybe I'm broken inside*, then let that thought pass.

On the couch downstairs in his den, he asks, "So why did you choose me?"

"I don't know," I say weakly. "You're a good-looking guy. You seemed normal—not rough like you would hurt me or anything."

"I'm flattered," he says with a smirk.

"I guess I just felt comfortable talking to you," I say, truthfully.

Luke's the first guy I've ever mentioned *The Incident* to. And he didn't flip out. "There's a steadiness about you," I add.

"A steadiness?" he asks.

"It's hard to explain," I shrug. "Something just kind of felt right."

Luke positions his body across mine and we kiss. It's not romantic, but like I said, it just feels right. There are no butterflies or heart palpitations, but I kiss him back like I always do and try to mean it.

"Let's leave this on," he says, tugging the bottom of my blouse. "It looks good."

When we're both bottomless, Luke grabs the lubricant from the side table and squeezes some out. It makes an embarrassing farting noise so I giggle. I hold still as he rubs some onto me. I don't tingle. My muscles clench up, but I want him to go on.

"Why don't we try standing this time?" he says, putting

the condom on. He positions me so that my hands are on the arm of the couch as he stands just behind me. "I won't go any further than you want," he assures me.

"Okay," I inhale with a nod.

Luke holds on to my hips, and I can feel my body resisting him right away. I thrust toward the couch away from him as he moves in after me.

"Do you want to take a breather?" he asks, after about ten minutes of me pulling myself away.

"No," I say. "I'm trying to make it work."

"Do you want me to put on any particular music? Tell me whatever you want to make it easier," he says.

"Just go again," I say, anxiously biting my lip. But eventually he gives up and *The Great Barrier of Grief* keeps holding court.

I'm putting my shorts back on when I see that he's not putting his pants back on.

"Do you mind if I do this?" he asks, as he starts to slowly rub himself up and down.

Out of shock, my mouth drops open. I close it right away. "Yeah. No," I say, breathlessly.

So I sit down and watch as he looks at me and brings himself to orgasm. And I don't know why, but it's freakishly hot. I've never seen it before—not even in soft porn. It's so weird what our bodies do... and what they won't.

ANIMALS

My oldest sister is in the hospital again so the tubes can force-feed her, or at least that's what I think I overheard. I don't ask many questions because my mom's so upset all the time. I don't want to set her off.

The two just younger than me are always screaming and fighting. I'm glad my brother is now picking on my younger sister and not me anymore. I'm afraid what I might do if he breaks down my door again. He's an angry kid, and he's always been for some reason. Kids always give him a hard time for being fat, but he deals with it by eating more food—maybe to show it doesn't bother him. Then he takes it out on us. My sister stands up to him better than I do. She gives it back just as bad with biting words that I'm too afraid to say.

The sister next older than me loves the baby so much. Sometimes she pretends he's her and her boyfriend's baby. It's kind of odd, but at least it means I don't have to babysit so much.

I feel bad for the brother next up from the baby. He was the baby for seven years, and my other brother is always picking on him. He's a gentle soul. I've always had a soft spot for him because he's quiet—like me.

The animals don't see me the way the rest of the family sees me. Maybe they see through my skin. I spend a lot of time with them these days. We connect in a way that allows me to feel there's still some good in the world—and maybe some good left in me.

I petted Maggie downstairs in the playroom today for what must've been hours. The light from the windows shone down onto us in the dark room. He looked up to me as if to squint, *thank you*, as I'd stroke him from the top of his head down to the end of his fluffy tail. It feels almost ritualistic petting the cats this way. We get into a rhythm of petting and purring, and it slowly fills the empty space.

Maybe it's the movement, our ritual, that reveals that I feel more like them than my brothers and sisters. The dogs and the cats and me—we were all brought in from the outside, one at a time, to fill a void we couldn't quite fill. And then another arrived. No wonder we all need so much reassurance that we're worth something to someone. It's so easy for my parents to neglect us—the quiet ones, not born from them, who are lucky to have a home and basic needs met. The ones who need nothing from the quick glances at us. Not when the baby's crying or my sister's dying, anyway.

Truth is, if I knew how to act like a normal person, how to say what I need the way everyone else does, I'd have made things a lot easier for everyone. Even the way *The Incident* happened—it wouldn't have happened if I didn't need just one person to recognize me for something I want to be seen as, something other than just *the Chinese-looking girl*.

I think because I've never been the pretty one, I've always felt good about the things I can do—like write songs. If I couldn't be seen as that kind of special, I wanted so desperately to be seen as some kind of special. I got it wrong though.

But now at least I have Luke as my distraction, my goal. It's kind of messed up that I need this to happen so badly. I never thought I'd be wanting to have sex, unmarried at seventeen, but life is just different now.

The fifth time he picks me up and I sashay toward his car, I pray that *The Great Barrier of Grief* will break down. A quick kiss in the car with a compliment and we're heading across a couple of towns to Luke's house again.

"I got us some wine coolers," he says, pulling a couple out from the fridge. "I was thinking maybe they'd help you relax."

"Oh," I say. "Good idea."

We sit on the oversized tan couch sipping on bottles of booze. There's a silence we're now comfortable in that we don't rush to fill. I try to listen to the lyrics floating out of the radio while the cold drink sweats in my hand. After about one and a half of them, I feel different. There's a numbness that begins to fade away and another one that slyly slides into its place.

"I like these." I smile at Luke, holding the bottle up.

"I thought you might," he says, smiling back.

Soon enough, we're tasting sweet berries off one another's tongues and lips. I marvel at how tangy it tastes off of him.

Kissing him feels different this time—probably from the alcohol, but I think I like it better. It's like I can actually feel him.

With our clothes strewn about the floor, Luke's sitting on the couch, rolling down a condom. "I thought we could try it another way this time," he says.

"Okay," I say. "How?"

"Why don't you get on top of me?" he says. "That way you can control it."

I'd never thought of doing it like that. It kind of scares me a little. I think about what he said—about me having control—and decide it's a worth a shot.

I kneel on either side of Luke, facing him, afraid to move.

"I'll help you," he says, guiding my hips until our bodies barely touch.

"Now it's up to you," he says, releasing me, resting his hands on my thighs.

I let myself drop onto him and quickly buck up from the contact five or six times. I breathe deeply, in and out, take another swig, and feel myself relax as I try it again. As I feel him enter me just a little, I freeze, holding steady.

"You can do this," he whispers. "You're nearly there."

"Help me," I say lowly, needing his strength to push me down.

And slowly, very slowly, I endure the sharp pain as it grows stronger and harder inside me. That pain, so familiar but so very different. I look down at Luke's approving face, and I know I can do this. I relax into it a little more. I move halfway up and down maybe five times before I have to stop.

"It's okay," he says to me, as I lift off of him.

METAMORPHOSIS

There's a slight spring in my step in school the next day. People are looking at me differently. I see Samantha and Kellie in the hall and I tell them, "I did it," with a beaming smile.

"You did?" they say in unison.

I nod and they smile with a look of surprise. They don't even know about *The Incident*, I don't think, but always noted my discomfort around the topic of sex.

"I'm impressed," Kellie says.

"You're a woman now," Samantha smirks.

In the background, Marianne comes into focus. She's standing at her locker listening to us. She looks away shyly as my eyes catch hers.

I know Marianne disapproves. Marianne is my old best friend. We were so close in middle school, but we drifted apart. As I got more involved in going into the city for music, her dad got wary of me and the city kids I was hanging around. I want to hug her and tell her that her dad was right to protect her, but I just look away.

There's an energy that buzzes in my blood, now that I've made it happen. I've got more confidence in myself. I make jokes in class and hold my head higher, no longer afraid to look at people.

Having sex with Luke is changing me as a person. I can hear my dead cells hit the floor as I almost too quickly morph into a new version of myself. A less pathetic girl. A braver girl. Someone I'm not ashamed to be.

I'm almost surprised when Luke calls again. A part of me thought he'd stop once we broke through.

"Want to come over again on Tuesday?" he asks.

"Okay," I say, hearing the smile in my own voice.

"You sound different," he says, hearing it too. "Have a good day?"

"Yeah," I say. "For a change."

"Good. You sound better happy," he says.

When I watch TV later that night, I click through and come across a rape scene. I forward past it and then click back, mute the volume, and watch. It's not graphic but it infers plenty. There's something horrifying yet exhilarating about it. I feel guilty but touch myself a little under the sheets. I'm careful not to move too much since one of the little monitors in the kitchen feeds from the camera in my room.

I force stop. I don't let myself get too carried away. I'm too cautious and always hyper-conscious of the world around me. And I feel like there must be something evil— something awfully disturbing inside me for that scene to have aroused me. Especially after what I've been through.

* * *

My sister's back from the hospital again. She's now on a special diet that consists of eating the same damn thing every meal. It's the only thing she'll eat because they promised her it won't put any fat on her body. It's supposed to help her build muscle. You can see bones through her clothes, but her fear of fat goes a long way.

This disease has made her weird. To eat, she has to set the same spot at the table with a place mat, spoon, and the exact same bowl in position. Our troublemaker brother has been fucking with her by moving her spoon when she turns away. When she turns back to see things amiss, she screeches in this piercingly high, deafening tone. I don't know why he does it to her—to us. I think he's jealous that she's so skinny and he's still fat. He makes fun of how skinny she is while she heats up that orange mush she calls Indian pudding. The smell of it turns my stomach, but I don't want to say anything to stop her from eating it.

I go down the hall to the other end of the house to find one of my younger brothers. I stop when I hear my mother's muffled voice. I push the door open and kneel on the carpet, quietly, in the doorway. She's crying and slams the phone, picks it up again and dials a number.

"You don't understand. She's dying!" She stifles a yell. "She doesn't look fine! She needs to eat! Please," she says, I assume to my sister's crazy boyfriend, "I'm begging you. You need to tell her she'd look better if she eats or she'll die!"

She hangs up the phone and cries again so I leave her,

not wanting to get caught. I head into the quiet brother's room and sit on the bed with a cat while I watch him play video games. I play a couple rounds of Enduro against him when he's done.

* * *

Tuesday can't come soon enough to rescue me from familial insanity. I don't even want to hang out with the girls much these days. I still feel like I'm two feet above them, as stuck up as that sounds. They have their real problems too. Kellie found sex toys in her mother's bedroom, and Samantha's dad verbally abuses her in front of her friends. Yet still, they know a threat but not the promise fulfilled. And I hope they never know just how bad things can be.

When Luke picks me up, he takes a different route than usual.

"Are we not going to your place?" I ask.

"We are," he says. "I thought we'd get some ice cream first. There's this place that makes their own. You can even see the cows out back."

"Alright," I say, staring out the window at all the normal people and what I imagine to be their normal homes. I don't tell him ice cream gives me bellyaches.

I end up getting a chocolate-vanilla swirl, so I have to eat it fairly quickly before it melts. Luke gets his in a bowl and eats with a spoon, keeping his eyes on me. I can feel his stare through my hair as I twist my head to lick around the swirl.

"Do you like it?" he asks.

I turn to him and nod. "Mmm."

"It looks like you're enjoying it," he says.

And from then on I know what I'm doing. I take my time licking from bottom to top, lapping up little drips down the cone. I can hear when Luke's heart nearly stops.

Back in the cozy basement of his house, he hands me a wine cooler. I smile as I take it and feel the tart mix of the berry and the residue of the ice cream collide on my tongue. Luke puts on some music, and I dance around a little, exploring my braver persona.

"So this is the new you?" he says coyly. But I can tell he's not trying to knock me.

"Maybe," I say, smiling up toward the ceiling as I slowly find the beat of the song.

"I like it," he says approvingly. He sits on the couch and swigs his drink.

"Are you gonna join me or just watch like a perv?" I ask, grinning.

"I'm gonna watch like a perv," he says, bemused.

I dance as I finish the first bottle. Luke fetches me another before I even have to ask.

"Are you trying to get me drunk, Luke?" I ask with a smirk.

"Just relaxed," he says with a wink.

We drink and we kiss, tasting booze on each other. I dance, and he stands next to me swaying a little. And just like he's never pushed me further than I want to go, I let him sway a little offbeat.

I find myself straddling him again on the couch the way we did it last time. I was foolish enough to think it'd be easy this time, but it doesn't matter that it's already been broken through. *The Great Barrier of Grief* is still fighting. I reach for my wine cooler and combat it with another swig.

After a few tries it starts to work. It doesn't feel good physically, but I keep telling myself the more I do it, the better it will get. I think I make it all the way down this time too. I last about five minutes before having to stop. As I tell him I need to pull him out, he comes as I lift off of him.

Luke gets out of the car to open my door and gives me a quick kiss on the lips. I hear him drive away as I enter the house and the sounds of the Vaniti's fade in full-force.

I brush my teeth and slip into my room, throwing a shirt over the camera as I change into a T-shirt and workout pants. I do my stretches and crunches before getting into bed.

Our black Lab-mix Mandi pushes the door open with her nose, and I get up to close it behind her. I spoon her on my futon and we fall asleep.

WHITE NOISE

Things are getting pretty intense at home. My parents are fighting more than usual because apparently there's money missing from my dad's business. A lot of money. It's been going on for years, so my mom stepped in to take a look at the accounting books that my dad's sister's been handling.

"Everything's written in code! I can't make sense of any of it!" Mom yells.

My dad's not able to admit that my aunt—his only sibling—could be the one behind it. It's creating an ugly, unspoken ultimatum for my dad to choose between his sister and his wife. But either way, they can't come up with hundreds of thousands of dollars that just seemed to vanish over the last few years.

As with all the tension that goes on in this house, I avoid it like the plague. I've got plenty of my own shit to deal with and am just happy when I'm not in the center of the shit storm.

Mom barges into my room and asks, "Will you help your sister with her report? She can't seem to figure it out and she needs help!"

I nod my head. She throws the report on my dresser and slams the door, getting back into it with Dad.

I look at my sister's report. It's full of grammatical errors and completely disjointed. I start to mark it up and then sigh as I take out a pen and paper to rewrite it for her. Neither she nor the angry brother can ever seem to do their writing or art projects. I'm pretty sure it's because they know my mom will get me to do them. Even so, at this point I've stopped protesting. Otherwise it's a big argument, and I end up doing them anyway. I've tried sitting with them to guide them through it, but they have no patience for that. I have to believe their teachers are smart enough to know that I'm the one doing it, as they'd remember my work. But who knows? People turn a blind eye for convenience.

Seven kids. Why would anyone do that? In rare, soothing moments, if we're sitting petting cats, I'll ask my mother why she wanted so many kids. But instead of answering, as always, she poses another question.

"Who would you get rid of?" she says. I bite my tongue with a few ideas.

She has one sister, and they don't get along. They're either fighting or not speaking. And now that my dad's only sister is a potential problem, our big family is a lot smaller. I kind of liked when we had places to go at holidays or people to come by. Now it's just us without anyone else's dysfunctions to temporarily distract us.

And it's not that I think our family is particularly bad.

I'm sure we're no worse than anyone else but our family problems are amplified from the sheer number of us. The more mouths, the more sounds, the more problems. There's always someone to worry about.

To be honest, I'm kind of stressed out about my oldest sister. Last night I had a freaky dream that her head was off her body in the changing room at the Y. She was standing naked near the showers, all boney, and her head was on the plastic waffle floor as she spoke nonsense to me. She wouldn't believe me that her head was unattached.

What will happen if we lose her?

I don't want to think about it.

She's the one who taught me to draw, one night up in Maine. She always had a lot of talent, and I wanted to be able to do what she did. She used to sing too. But all those things about her have disappeared with the weight.

I hear her running in place in the bathroom across the hall from my room. Sometimes I knock on the door just to get her to stop for a minute. And sometimes she giggles to herself, but it's beyond humor. I think she's gone nuts.

The loud, angry brother's so mean to the quiet one. He screams his name at the top of his lungs to come in and change the channel, to be the human remote. It's totally mental.

So much noise. So much noise all the time.

In my room, there's a sort of book closet four feet up the wall. I turned it into a small fort. It's plastered with *Teen* and *Tiger Beat* cutouts of Corey Haim in leather jackets and on motorcycles. I hung a curtain just inside the doors so the little crevice between them won't let much light in. And then I fed a cord through the hinge for a lamp.

I sit in there to get quiet when I need it. I have to sit with my legs crossed at a certain angle to fit but it works. I used to practice singing in private in here, but now I just go for the peace. I don't even bother turning on the light half the time. I shut my eyes and go blank.

Luke calls later in the day, and I lay back on my bed, cradled by a giant stuffed white lion that was won by a friend at a carnival in Maine.

"Hey, Millie," he says.

Just as I'm about to respond, my brother picks up another line and yells, "Get off the phone!"

"I'm talking," I tell him.

"Get off the fucking phone!" he yells.

"No, I—" A piercingly loud *beeeeeeeeee…* drowns us out as he holds numbers down. I slam the phone down and sulk to myself about what an absolute jerk he is.

He just lives to make our lives miserable, and I was always so nice to him. To this day, I'm the only one in the family who's never called him fat. And I swear he does these things just to see if he can break me. He wants to know the whole world sucks that bad so he can—*what?* —I don't know.

It's not like being fat is the worst thing in the world. He's so self-centered that he can't see what it's like for other people—people like me. I'm the one he calls the ugly chink to his friends. I can't ever lose being chinky-looking. He can call me all kinds of names to try to awaken the beast inside me, but I refuse to call him fat.

I have dreams that someone's trying to kill me. I always have—even way before *The Incident*. This one recurring dream is of a man dressed in the typical robber's outfit—all in black with the face mask—hunting me down with a knife. Each time he nearly sticks me, I manage to turn on the wall, rolling down the long hall in our house. No one wakes up to try to save me, and I barely escape every time. Then I really wake, aware of every little sound in the otherwise quiet house.

I don't think my brother would really try to kill me. I don't think the dream's about him, but I've suffered from nightmares like this my whole life.

Something's trying to kill me though. I just feel it. Sometimes I wish it would try a little harder.

I think my brother wants me to think he would or could kill me. He even threatens the life of the cat that he loves. He threatens everyone. I think he wants us to think he has all this power because in reality, he doesn't have any. He doesn't stand up to the kids at school. I suppose we're easier targets.

My dad's got this odd obsession with protecting the house. There's the alarm system, the cameras in our rooms and the driveway—oh, and the front door. Every room has an intercom system. It all looks like we have so much to protect. The kids at school think we're rich, yet I keep hearing how poor we are now.

I think my parents want us to look rich. They bought a stretch limousine for Christ's sake. And when I didn't know how to respond, they said I should call my friends and tell them how excited I was. I don't think they know that this perception they're creating would make people want to break in. Maybe it's partly why my aunt steals from us—thinking we have so much to go around?

The next day after school, I call Luke and apologize for

my brother being an ass. He laughs it off and wants to pick me up later on. I couldn't possibly want anything more than to escape for a few hours with him.

Down in Luke's den, I suck down the wine cooler as fast as I can. I haven't really gotten the taste for alcohol much, but wine coolers are kind of like candy. I like the tension it lifts and the ones it creates. I'm able to stop focusing so much on the annoyances in life and just be in the moment with him.

We talk about music a little. We're both into this new grunge alternative thing that's happening. He rubs my knee now and then, and we smile at each other. I'm starting to feel a slight chemistry building. The more I see him, the less numb I am when around him.

He's less shy when I'm dancing now. He even comes up to join me, holding my hips, swaying with me from side to side. Our thing is so uncomplicated. It's just what we do, what we need.

When we do it this time, I can feel myself give in a little more. It still hurts the whole time it's going on, but in my head, I really like what we're doing. I like choosing to do this with him and him wanting to do it with me. I can tell that he really likes my body, and he's good with it. He's not crude or anything.

"Did you come?" he asks me this time.

"I don't know," I say, truthfully. I don't know what coming is like for a girl.

"It's okay," he says. "Someday you will, and it'll be all the better."

And from what I've overheard from the kids at school, I'm surprised by how easily he takes it. Some girls say they fake orgasms just so guys don't take it personally. They must be with lesser men. Or maybe they're more caring than I am.

I see a Victoria's Secret catalog in his kitchen. "This yours?" I ask with a smile.

"It's my sister's, but I flip through sometimes," he smirks.

I thumb through page after page of beautiful women half-dressed in satin and lace. I think I look for too long because Luke takes notice.

"You like that stuff?" he asks.

I nod my head. Secretly, I've been going to lingerie stores to stock up on sexy clothes and hide them in my room. I put them on in the mirror sometimes in the middle of the night and it looks good. I don't know why, but I'm fascinated by lingerie. It's like a costume. I can pretend to be pretty.

"Would you ever wear something like that for me?" he asks shyly.

I nod my head again with an awkward smile.

OVEREXPOSURE

I don't know how to explain how something that doesn't feel particularly good can turn me on. It's such a strange contradiction that happens when we have sex. Yet I can't get enough of it.

I think I'm starting to get a little too fond of Luke, and that worries me a little. In less than five weeks, my whole family will be going to Maine again as we do every summer. It'll be weird without him. And he'll probably find someone else.

In the mirror attached to the back of my bedroom door, I watch myself slink into the white lingerie that I'm thinking of wearing for him. There's just something about white. It vibrates off my skin and my nearly black hair. It's frilly and sexy. A prostitute would never wear this. Somehow that thought makes it right.

I don't love him. At least I don't think I do. I couldn't tell you what love really is or feels like, but I doubt that it's what we have. Despite all that, I don't feel guilty for what I'm doing with Luke. He's one hell of a do-over. He makes me feel good about myself when I'm with him, and that's more than I can say for anyone else.

When I get everything laced up and step back to see myself a little better, the door pops open and whacks me on the nose.

"Get out!" I scream at the quiet brother's little head, which pulls back. He looks sad and shocked when he sees and hears me.

I'm not a screamer. There are too many of those in my house. It's quite rare when I yell, and I instantly feel sorry for it. But I'm also embarrassed that he's seen me like this and afraid it may traumatize him. After all, the loud brother's into making him watch porn already. I don't want to imagine what he's thinking.

I scurry around to put on the outfit I'd chosen that will hide what I have on underneath. I fall down onto my bed, face smashed to the pillow, and wish I had the balls to yell. But of course, I don't. I've reached my quota for the month.

At Luke's house I take off my outer clothes in the laundry room to reveal my white frills at once. He is visibly pleased when I come out to see him. He looks like a kid who got what he wanted for Christmas.

"Let me see you," he smiles, turning me around a little, soaking it all in. "You look hot," he says.

"Did you get any wine coolers?" I ask, suddenly too much in the moment.

Luke nods and takes my hand, moving toward the fridge. He twists the caps off and hands me a bottle. As I let the cold berry flavor splash down my throat, I start to regain some courage.

Soon enough, I'm leaning over the couch, and we're having sex like they do it on Skinamax. It's sensual, slow, and in control. It doesn't feel good down there, but it feels good up here in my mind where I spend all my time anyway. Luke is loving it, and that makes me love it too.

I feel a little shy when it's over somehow, as Luke is obviously worked up more than ever. There's a rawness to him that I haven't yet seen until now. There's a look on his face that's more man than boy, and it makes me a little uncomfortable.

"You okay?" he asks, collapsed on the couch.

I nod my head and move into the laundry room to dress. I resurface with a slight smile, trying to look comfortable, but he can tell that I'm not.

"Was that okay for you? Too much?" he asks.

I say, "Yeah. No," and keep on my half-smile.

"Okay," he says. "You can always tell me, during, you know."

"I know," I say, nodding at him. It didn't feel weird until after.

Luke slips into his pants and shirt and rests before putting his socks on.

"I love that you wore that for me," he says, patting my thigh.

I finish my wine cooler and stop feeling quite as awkward inside.

Back home, I head into the bathroom to change so no one barges in on me this time. I brush my teeth and go into my room to do my stretches and sit-ups.

When I was in gymnastics, I did so many sit ups that

those muscles are softening now and look a little bumpy. They never told us we'd have to keep working out as hard forever—even after we decided to quit.

Samantha and Kellie call me on three-way and want to know where this bitch has been. They like to use the words bitch, slut, and whore, affectionately. I never dug that whole thing but go along with it.

"You've been spending all your time with Luke," Kellie says. "You never wanna hang out with us."

"Yeah, whore," Samantha says, chiming in.

"Well, what's going on? Anything good?" I ask, from under the shadow of my white lion.

"Yeah. Come to this party with us on Saturday," Kellie says. "There'll be lots of cute boys there."

"That's if you can peel yourself away," Samantha jokes.

"Alright," I say, hoping it'll make them feel better. It also crosses my mind that it could be a preventative measure from being depressed when it comes to leaving Luke this summer.

Kellie and Samantha are nice, pretty girls. One's blonde and the other's brunette. They mean well, I really do believe that deep down, but somehow trouble always finds them. I'm still reminded from my parents every now and then about the time they brought a car full of strange boys to my house who robbed us while my parents were at dinner. None of us saw it happen. We could hardly believe it when we saw things missing once they'd left. They were good, and I caught so much shit for it. It's the one time I'd wished the surveillance cameras recorded.

Now when I'm going out with Kellie and Samantha, I always have to throw in the name of another girl my parents like, such as Marianne—who doesn't even care for the other two. They're usually too busy to press much, though.

I put on my little jean shorts and a white netted sixties blouse with daisies and bell sleeves. I wear black Doc Martens to balance out all the femme.

I'm in a car full of girls who look hot with the stereo blasting as we swig from bottles in the back. Our cute red-headed friend and alpha girl with huge boobs are with us. We're like a traveling wet dream.

As usual, we have a hard time finding the party. Kellie is always sighing at Samantha's driving. They're like an old married couple—the way they bicker. We pull into a convenience store parking lot for Samantha to get cigs and directions.

And just as Samantha's through the door, a cop car pulls up alongside us with the sirens blaring. We all duck down in the car, instinctively on top of the booze. Then we look at each other wide-eyed and mouth, "Samantha!"

Samantha opens the car door a minute later with a pack of cigarettes like it's no big deal. We ask her what happened and she says someone hit the button by mistake. She says, "I was like, 'Relax! I'm just buying butts!'" And we all laugh as she peels back out onto the street.

By the time we get to the right house we're a couple hours late which means everyone's already wasted. There are kids smoking weed, flopped over on the couch, and abandoned card games as kids slump forward on the table. And then I spot Luke.

"Hey, what's Luke doing here?" I ask no one, heading over to where he is on the floor. Some of his friends are trying to help him up onto a chair.

"What happened to him?" I ask, amazed at the sight before me. I've never seen him so ill composed. It's almost as if it can't be the same person.

"He had one too many!" yells one of the boys. "Didn't ya?" he says, slapping Luke on the cheek. I want to pull his hand away but I don't.

"He lost the game, so he had to drink all the shit in the middle," says another.

"Oh, Kings," I say, at least relieved for an explanation.

I leave them there and turn around to find the girls, who are obviously disappointed at what we've found. None of the possibly cute boys are even sober enough to appreciate our outfits.

"What a waste," sighs Kellie, looking around.

"Yarrrr," says Samantha, like a pirate.

We laugh, grab the others, and head back to the car with our booze. We pass around some bottles of things I've never heard of before. It's a way to concede a letdown, I suppose.

I'm still thrown by the image of Luke as he was, so I drink with the girls to get it off my mind. We belt out a song in unison so loudly that we think you can't hear our drunken mistakes.

I stumble out of the car and hit the grass for a moment before steadying myself back up. The girls are all laughing, and I'm laughing too as I shush them so not to wake anyone. My parents are probably home and in bed already. The last thing any of us needs is for them to come out.

I miraculously make my way through the door, up the stairs, and into my room where I struggle to undress. I just tear everything off clumsily, feeling dizzy and confined. I tuck into bed with a fluffy stuffed dog and then realize that I have to pee.

When I know I won't be able to hold it any longer, I shift myself up and figure I can run across the hallway to the bathroom since everyone's asleep. And that's no problem. But unfortunately, as I spin to shut the door and miss twice, I spin myself into the tub that has doors that clank and thunder as I land clumsily inside it.

My mother's voice from next door bellows, "What the *hell* is going on out there!"

Oh shit.

I scramble out of the tub, shut the door, and pee as quickly as possible. I run back across the hall and tuck myself into bed with my heart pounding through my chest.

The next day I wake with dried puke on my little stuffed dog and memories of Luke passed out cold.

SEX AND LIES

Luke's friend Micah is sitting in the driver's seat of a red T-Top Firebird while Luke waits outside for me with the door open. I see him nod at Micah as I strut my way toward them in a black flowery A-line skirt and a black bodysuit.

"You look gorgeous," he says, pecking me on the lips before I slide into the backseat. And to my surprise, instead of climbing into the front he slides in back with me, shutting the door behind him.

Micah's one of the boys who was at the party, and I've seen him a few times before. He was there the night we all met. He's a decent looking guy, but he's nothing like Luke. He wears his insecurities on his sleeve.

He puts the radio on so loud that we can't possibly hear one another. He whips us onto the road. There's no chance of asking Luke what was up the other night or even learn if he knew I was there. So instead, I go along with the make-out session that he slides us into with ease.

Luke's got one hand on my thigh and is holding my shoulders up with the other. It would be romantic if the heavy classic rock wasn't so loud, but I enjoy the passion of the moment. He surprises me with this and the adventure of the unknown turns me on.

I notice Micah's sunglasses peering in the rearview mirror now and then, but it doesn't bother me. I feel sexy and free with myself gazing up to the blur of the sky through the trees. Luke's not at all distracted, and I lose myself in his focus.

We take the long way to Luke's house and Micah waves goodbye as we head inside. Down in the den, we're sipping wine coolers in between kissing and playful petting. Luke pours a little out onto my chest and kisses it off, looking up at me with those pale blue eyes and long lashes. I tilt my head back and close my eyes, held up by his arm around my waist. And when I open my eyes for half a second, I swear I see something moving outside.

"There's someone out there," I say to Luke, who's not too alarmed.

"There is?" he says, looking up half-heartedly.

"I thought I saw jeans and shoes," I say, as the den is mostly underground. "It doesn't matter." And we carry on as we were.

Half-dressed and bent over the couch, it's starting to feel good for the first time for me. There's an extra twinge of excitement in the air, and I breathe it in slowly through parted lips and teeth. It's close to ten times now, I think, and I was starting to worry that it'd never feel good. But here I am in the moment with him, on the verge of my first orgasm.

I can feel Luke affected by my climb and the tension continues to build inside me. I go first, and he follows right behind. We collapse forward, bodies moving by breaths. As we stir to get ourselves back together, I see a flash of movement outside once again.

I point clumsily to the window across the room, and Luke nods while pulling up his jeans. He goes to the window and looks up and around with a shrug, comes back, and we catch our breath on the couch.

"How did it feel?" he asks, eyes only half-open, gazing at me.

"Unreal," I say truthfully.

"It'll only get better," he smirks, tapping my thigh.

"Definitely worth the wait," I sigh.

As I lay in bed at night, I feel guilty. It's a strange brand of guilt, and I've felt it before but can't quite place when or where. It's just familiar, awkward, and uncomfortable to be in my own skin. I didn't feel it at Luke's, nor in his or Micah's car, but I cringe at the way it slips over me now.

All my life I've been told that sex is a thing only the bad girls like. It's dirty and cheap if not shared between a couple that has promised their lives to one another. My dad says he's only ever been with Mom, but I saw the way she squirmed when he said it to me. And to tell you the truth, it grossed me out.

We're not even supposed to imagine that sex between a married couple is ever pleasurable. It's laughed about on sitcoms and movies as non-existent or lame. It's either like that or slutty. So when is sex supposed to be good—to feel good just because it does?

Sex is such a huge thing. It's like the difference between

whether you're marriage material or a whore. It's the distinction between being whole or broken. It's such a taboo topic in our culture, yet we can't escape it. We're both intrigued and frightened by it. Men can show it off, and women have to bury it in a diary and then burn the pages later.

Sex isn't supposed to be fair. Or is that love? Sex and love are supposed to be intertwined, so how the fuck should I know?

All I know is that sex has changed the way I'm seen by my family, my school, and my friends. And now it's changing the way I'm starting to see myself. Is it wrong that I prefer this version of me to the past? Does that make me an unmarriable, dirty whore?

And what's the difference if I like it or not? After *The Incident*, I'm tarnished already. Shouldn't there not be a way to make that worse? Shouldn't I get a pass and at least be able to take something that shitty and twist it into something I can actually enjoy?

THE PHONE CALL

There's been a strange car parked down the road a few nights this week. I gaze out onto our street from my bedroom window, every sober night since *The Incident*. It's usually there really late—like after eleven—but I never see anyone get out. I don't want to admit it to myself because I don't want to believe I've gone crazy, but I have suspicions that sane girls wouldn't have. I never see when the car leaves either. It's a mystery that haunts me throughout the day.

In class, they're all reading as I gaze out the window. My teacher glances across the room and sighs when she sees me. I pretend not to see her as she pretends not to notice me.

I wonder if it's *him* in that car, scoping the house, taking notes on our comings and goings. My dad leaves for work at five in the morning, so maybe he knows that already. It's not like my dad is a big guy or anything—quite the contrast. But somehow I imagine if someone were to cause harm on a family, he would plan it for when the father's not there.

I wonder if he knows what time I'm home from school and when my mom's alone with the baby. I wonder if he sees when the mail comes and if he knows the hiding spot near the door where I've hidden before, just to scare people for fun.

The ways are endless. I find myself wishing I were an only child because then I'd have less people to be responsible for hurting. I've always tossed that thought around in my head before, but I do so now more than ever.

I'm sitting in my room on the floor when the phone rings later that evening.

"Hello?" I say.

There's a silence. And then a "Hi."

It's a voice I remember, one I thought I'd somehow forgotten. But here it is whispering in my ear again.

"Hi," I say, unsure of what next.

I can almost hear a faint high-pitched tone far away in the background; the silence is that thick, and I'm listening that hard.

"You know who this is?" he says.

"Yeah," I say, afraid to ask what he wants.

"I just wanted to tell you that... I didn't realize what happened that day," he says.

I don't understand what he means.

"I didn't know, like..." He sighs in quiet frustration. "I thought what we did—that you liked it. I thought that's just how it be."

I bite my tongue, not wanting to lose it and scream all

the reasons why he should know that not to be the case. But instead, my body defies me again as I sit stiffly and silently in place.

"I heard from some people what I did to you. Look—I'm not gonna hurt you. I just wanna say dat," he says. "I'm not like dat, how I was back then."

I nod to myself, clutching onto the phone. I throw a wall up in my mind so not to let all the visions from that night come rushing into view. The gun, the mattress, the car, the others...

"So, um," he says, cutting through the silence, "I didn't mean it, I guess."

"Uh huh," I say, barely.

"You forgive me?" he says, with what seems like a childish pout.

"Yeah," I say, without letting myself think of all the things I'd have to forgive if I really mean it. There's too much—just too much—but I can't tell him that. Even as I hear the need in his voice and want to deny him any peace because I'll never know peace again, that's all I can say: *Yeah*.

"I 'ppreciate dat," he says.

"Uh huh," I say. "Okay, bye."

"Bye," he says, and hangs up.

I listen to the tone of the open line for a few moments before hanging up.

I look at the phone in my hand—the ridiculous red high-heeled shoe phone that's come in handy when my dad's taken away my other phones in the past. I slip it into my closet, disguised among the other shoes. Then I marvel at the weight of what happened just then while that ridiculous thing was pressed up to my head.

I wake the next morning with memories of the call, unsure if it was real or a dream.

DISSIDENTS

"Did you know he was watching?" I ask through the phone.

"In the car I did, yeah," says Luke, "but not in the house. I yelled at him for that."

"It's okay," I tell him. "I mean, I wouldn't want him making a regular thing of it but I kind of liked it—him not knowing that I knew he was there. I don't know why, but there was something about it."

"Huh," Luke contemplates. "It's kind of gross, thinking about him watching us do it. I've known him most of my life."

"I could see that," I say. "But to me, he's practically a stranger."

"I liked making out with you in the car though," says Luke. I hear him grinning through the phone.

"Me too," I say, thinking about it. I start breathing a little heavily.

"Are you... touching yourself?" asks Luke, with a voice

full of shock.

"So what if I am?" I say, thinking about it.

"Hmmm," he says, panting a little now too.

"Are you touching *yourself*?" I ask.

"I could," he says.

I tuck into my closet so I can barely move, but at least I'll have warning if someone comes in.

"We've gotta be careful in case someone picks up another phone," I say, breathing deeply.

"I guess we'll be quiet then," he flirts.

There's nothing but intervals of light moans of pleasure from each of us for minutes.

"When you come, be silent," I whisper. "That way if someone picks up, they won't hear you."

"Okay," he moans. "It'll be any second."

And his sighs start to beat a little faster, so mine rise to meet his. And then silence. We both climax so quietly that it can't be heard. It's what we don't hear that tells us it's happening. I never thought silence could turn me on so much.

"How was that?" I ask him.

"Almost as good as the real thing," he tells me.

I don't tell him mine was better.

* * *

I love petting Freddie, but he gets too excited and gives me love bites on the chin. I always have to stop to give him a time out. I've never seen a cat so happy to be petted. Honestly, it's a little bizarre.

Petting him on the stairs by the foyer, I lean back and

gaze up at the big chandelier. I don't know if the crystals are real or not, but I like how the sun hits them and makes little rainbows on the walls. When I drift off too far, Freddie always reaches up to my chin with his white-gloved paws.

Freddie's an interesting cat. He's not like the others. He has a favorite teddy bear that was meant for my baby brother but is now only his because of what he's done to it. The boys make jokes and the girls turn away when he kneads on top of the thing a little too precariously. It's hard to think about him as a sexual being, but I can't deny him love just because of what he likes to do.

I wonder if my parents would disown me if they knew what I did. They'd probably be disgusted and outraged. They'd take the door off my room again, for all the good that it does.

People talk about this thing called "unconditional love," but I can't imagine a love that's not conditional. How far might you be able to go while you still hold on to love for another? If your husband cheated on you and then killed someone, wouldn't you be crazy to continue to love him?

I hate to say it, but I don't have unconditional love for anyone. Well, except maybe the cats and the dogs, but I can't imagine them doing anything to make me stop loving them.

I don't really understand love and how it works.

My parents say they love each other, but they never stop fighting. They say they love us kids, but we're always doing something wrong. I don't know why they love us—that is, *if* they do. I'm not sure I'd still love me.

Sometimes for just a second, I wonder about my birth parents. I'm sure that they're dead, but if not, I don't think that I could love them. I don't even know them. Am I sup-posed to love them automatically just because I come from them? Maybe it's different if your family is your blood, but I guess that's something I'll never know.

All these things that we do as human beings... We're so good at hate but not so much at love. If anyone knew the things we do in private, would anyone love anyone?

My anorexic sister comes up the stairs where Freddie and I are sitting. She's pouting and wearing too much makeup. I can hardly see her actual face. I guess she's always being made fun of. I don't know why. She was beautiful un-til she got sick. I don't get how it happened that one day, she just decided to be a whole different person and let it destroy everything good that she had.

"Hi," she says in a mopey tone.

"Hi," I say, cautiously, as she walks up past us.

I'm turning into someone else too, but she doesn't know it. Nobody does. So I wonder if someday they'll look at me the way we looked at her and realize that I'm a whole different person. How much do they have to know about this new me? Privacy is something I don't get either, for obvious reasons.

I don't think I even know who I am. I was always trying to be the perfect daughter and like everyone else—white and good. I tried to blend. Maybe this is better—the way things turned out. I don't have to pretend anymore because they know.

I'm not one of them.

SMOOTH
LIKE ICE CREAM

There are posters on this guy's wall of women in logo biki-
nis, smiling with cans of beer. He's got a Budweiser blimp
floating in the corner of the room and license plates he's
stolen hung to the wall. He lives in the basement apartment of his parents' house, and they know we're all drinking down here. He says they don't mind. They'd rather him
do it at home.

I follow Samantha out to the front yard so she can
throw up. Both parents are smiling as they sit on the front
steps. I apologize for Samantha, and they just laugh it off
saying it's okay—that they've been there. These are the cool
parents I've heard about, sipping beers with their son's
friends half their age. I find it kind of depressing.

Back down in the mix of the party, I watch people
smoke weed and turn it down. I don't do drugs. It's a hard

line for me. Everyone just looks like idiots when they're high. Then again, they're probably idiots to begin with.

Some of the girls are hot. The boys are okay, but they're so immature. They try so hard to be loud and outrageous. It bores the shit out of me, but the other girls seem to like it.

Kellie's always got a couple of guys' attention wherever she goes. She sits on a black leather couch in short shorts and combats, flipping her natural blonde hair.

"What's up, bitch?" I hear some of the girls say.

I nod to them. Occasionally I give a friendly, "Slut," back.

All this posturing.

Looking around the room, I have an epiphany. Maybe I'm not so weird after all. None of these kids look like they know who they are. They're all trying to be something that they're not either.

I think of Luke and wonder where he could be. He doesn't know any of this crowd, so I don't imagine I'll see him tonight.

We're still keeping it cool, but something's changing for me. Our time is ending soon, and no matter how hard I try, it's hard to keep it from messing with me. I'm stressed about our upcoming separation.

"You alright?" he asked, the last time he picked me up to get ice cream.

I nodded and lied. "Totally," I said.

And I don't want to push him away before our natural ending, so I keep it to myself. This thing that we have was an arrangement that carried on longer than I'd expected. I didn't mean to like him. I didn't think that I could like any-one that way again. I guess I was wrong.

"Whore, are you gazing off into space?" Kellie shouts from across the room.

"Yeah, bitch, I'm just thinking about your mother," I say.

We all laugh, and someone throws me another beer. I let myself slip away from my thoughts and try to pretend everyone's so cool and funny.

I'm still shopping for lingerie. There's this velvet strapless bra that I've been wanting to get. I pass Marshalls in the mall and step back to see what else they have in there.

I've always loved Fossil watches. Because they sell them at the boutique I work at in Maine, I had a little collection before those boys robbed our house. I check out the men's styles and find a brown and a black one that I can't decide between for Luke. Flustered, I get both.

I've been working on a letter to give him when I say goodbye for the summer. It feels like it could be for forever, so I don't take it lightly. I imagine he'll have a girl when I get back in a few months.

It's the first thing I've written in a while that's not homework. It's more like a thank you letter than anything, and everything sounds kind of foolish. I can't recall how many times I've scrapped the whole thing. I just want him to know he means a lot to me but not too much. It's a fine line to tread.

My mother's already started packing things up for the summer. We always take too much shit. Since my dad's working seven days a week, all of the packing is left up to her and us. I leave my stuff till the last two days because I can't live with my things scattered and half-packed. I'm messed up enough as it is.

When Luke comes to pick me up later, I relish the walk toward him and his car. His skin's starting to brown nicely from the sun, and it makes his eyes pop even more. I realize as I'm walking how these moments-are among the very few that I have to look forward to.

"You look beautiful as always," he says, smiling while opening my door.

I mimic his smile and wait anxiously for him to appear on the other side of me. And when he does, I want to reach over and kiss him, but something stops me. I feel my courage retreat.

We're not lovers. We're not a couple, says a voice in my head. *What does he think of me as*, I wonder, knowing better than to ask.

Back in the den of his mom's house, I sit on the couch while he brings me a drink. It feels good going down but doesn't seem to work fast enough.

"Easy there," Luke smiles. "You're pretty thirsty today."

I smile awkwardly and proceed to finish the bottle. As I finish the second, things start feeling better.

"You're lucky I've stocked up," he says, handing me a third.

I take a swig from the bottle and put it down on the side table. I kneel on the couch to start kissing him. Reaching down to his thigh, I slide my way up to make sure I can feel my effect on him.

"You're wild today," he says with approval. And that's all I need.

I decide to try something different. I open his pants and pull him out of his boxers. I kiss around the top of it lightly while trying to keep an unpleasant memory at bay. I don't know what I'm doing, but he seems to like it. And it feels right to be doing this for him.

"Slowly," he says to me calmly. "Like you do with the ice cream." And so I try. I gag a little but figure it's like the first five times we tried intercourse—that things will get easier with practice. And I can't tell if it's because he's enjoying it too much or too little, but he pulls out a condom.

I climb on top of him on the couch once again, and it's nicer this time. It hurts less than usual. And there's something inside me that wants to be perfect for him. I want him to miss me while I'm gone and maybe even wait for me. I think about all this as I move a little faster, enduring the pain as it dulls, until all of a sudden it feels good—extraordinarily good.

I lean back as he holds on to my hips, and I let myself slowly unwind. All my wanting to be something special to someone—*to him*—it swirls through my body as I fall back over him. He takes me down to the floor as he comes, breathing heavier with a few moans.

And then silence, just silence again, and it's all that I want to hear.

INEVITABILITY

I don't understand why anyone wants me to sign their yearbook or why I bother giving mine to them. It's like when we used to go to church, and all of a sudden you find yourself shaking hands or hugging strangers. It's such an awkward tradition that always takes me by surprise. Pretending people mean more than they do is so odd.

To be honest, I could hardly give a shit, so I just end up copying what everyone else says about them being a cool kid who shouldn't ever change. It's all so ridiculous. None of us are cool, and I hope to fuck that we all change.

But I suppose, to be fair, I'm just bitter about this whole end-of-the-year thing. Another year I barely coasted by on C's and D's with nothing of importance to retain and put into practice. And while everyone stays here and builds memories with one another, I'm hoisted up and out of the town and plopped back down in Maine. Up there, everyone's been bonding all year. It's just me and the other seasonal residents—who everyone secretly loathes—to try to make the most of the transient summer. And, of course, there's the matter of leaving Luke.

When I first started seeing Luke, I didn't really worry whether he liked me or not. I mean, I was giving him un-complicated sex, so I figured that was enough. In all of my fucked-up-edness, there was confidence in that I had noth-ing to prove. Today, our final day, I feel nauseated over what I'm going to wear.

Does he like my hair better up or down?
Shorts, skirt, or a dress?

I tuck the wrapped watches and the letter I wrote him into my purse with care. Anxiety over whether he'll like ei-ther watch or think my letter is pathetic eats away at my nerves while I try to apply eyeliner. Nothing I do seems to feel right, so I sit back on the bed to try to catch up with myself for a second.

In a white off-the-shoulder ruffled crop top and egg-plant-colored high-waisted shorts, I saunter across the walkway toward the driveway to greet him. Standing by the car, he tells me, "You look stunning."

Luke takes me to our ice cream place. I wore my hair up on the sides thinking that he might. It should keep my hair out of the ice cream and give him a better view as he watches me savor it—which he does.

As much as he doesn't feel it or I try to deny it, there's static between us. I lick my soft-serve swirl while he spoons his, watching me out of the corner of his eye. I wonder to myself who else he'll be watching in my place the next time he wants ice cream and I'm three hours gone.

We don't say much. The music fills the air for us.

When he pulls up in front of his house and parks the car, I try not to stare at the house for too long. I want to etch it into my memory.

"You coming in?" he asks, and I scamper up to reach him.

Luke sets the mood with some music, and I feel comfortable enough to get the wine coolers from his fridge. I notice there's beer in there as well.

"Are you having a party?" I ask, contemplative.

"Nope, just stocking up," he says. "Micah might come over to watch the game later."

I push the nagging jealousy out of my head, not wanting to ruin our last time together.

I go down on him again, giving it everything I've got. I pretend it's the ice cream, like he said to me before, and smile when I see that it's working. I hear the condom packet tear open and stand up and unbutton my shorts, face-to-face with him.

"How do you want to do it this time?" I ask, too eager to please.

He turns me around and slips everything off. We do it every which way, changing it up as we go, the both of us feeling the desperation of finality. It's a little more raw this time, the way we move, the way we look at each other. I think to myself, *This is just what I want*, and I let that thought consume me. The power of getting what I want from this person fills me with a sense of entitlement. I spin him onto the couch, straddle his legs, and we both come exactly the same way it all began.

On the way home, I ask him to pull over into a parking lot.

"How come?" he asks.

"I want to give you something," I say, "without the driveway cameras on me."

"Okay," he says, and does what I ask.

Standing outside of the car, I take the wrapped presents out of my bag.

"You didn't have to do that," he says. Then he adds, "I didn't get you anything."

"It's okay," I tell him. I hadn't expected anything. He's given me all I wanted.

He unwraps the first one. "Oh, cool," he says, examining it. "Thanks so much. I like it." Then he unwraps the other one and, with surprise, exclaims, "*Another* watch. Wow, thanks."

Of course I feel so stupid. "I couldn't decide which one you'd like more," I say.

"I like 'em both. Good choices," he says. "You didn't have to get me anything."

An uncomfortable silence starts to push us apart, so I say, "So what happens now?"

"What do you mean?" he asks, and then a look comes over his face as if he's trying to solve a riddle. "I guess we say goodbye for now."

I nod my head, feeling overcome with sadness. I feel like such a pathetic little girl. "I guess we do," I say somberly.

"Maybe you can call me when you get back," he offers. I can see he's trying to make me feel better without making any promises. And I know it's better this way, but it's not what I want to hear. Somehow it feels like rejection.

I nod my head again, getting back into the car. He

climbs back in as well and continues on toward my house.

I lean in for a quick kiss in the driveway. Luke makes to get out to open the door for me, but I rest my hand on his arm to stop him. I pull the letter out of my purse and hand it to him.

"This is for you," I say. "Don't forget me."

While he's looking puzzled at the folded up paper in his hand, I get out of the car and walk away. I can't help but think, *How fitting that we end similarly to how we began—with a folded-up paper.*

The house is as loud as ever, and I'm grateful to be able to walk in unnoticed. Mandi follows me into my room, and I shut the door behind us. I spoon her, crying into her fur as silently as possible while my body convulses. I hug her tightly, and she just lets me soak her fur without looking for answers. I love that about her.

WELCOME TO MAINE

Being able to drive to Maine this year is so much better than being a passenger in the convoy. I'm one of four vehicles hauling north and am happy to have the quiet brother with me in the handed-down car. We blast *Blood Sugar Sex Magik* with the windows down, feeling like rock stars on the open road—until we hit the traffic at the tollbooths, that is.

In one of the cars on our left, there are four shirtless guys about my age. They take turns holding up paper plates with weird sayings on them, such as *Help me! I'm kidnapped!* And *We're all gonna die!* We laugh along with them, feeling as if we're all part of some cool indie flick.

I love having this time with my brother. Only in the car are we able to feel this friendship as equals, despite the six years between us. In the house, we pretty much duck our heads, but on our own in the car, we can laugh and be silly. We can shout along to raucous music with profanity, and no one can tell us not to. The three hours go faster than they ever have. I'm almost sorry when it ends and the dreaded unpacking of the cars begins.

But somehow it's always a comfort, returning to this house and finding things as we left them. Shorts I didn't bother to pack last fall sit in the same wooden drawer. That creepy clown my mother painted as a child still lurks inside my closet.

The air smells of low tide and spruce. The dogs are happily sniffing around outside. We bring the cats to the porch and shut the door so they don't escape while we rummage around.

Later on, as my mother vacuums the carpet, Mandi charges across the room toward the old high chair that she used to fit under. We laugh as her big ass and tail spill out while her head and paws tuck under for safety. It's endearing to see a dog who's so smart in so many ways misjudge something as obvious as her own size.

I suppose Maine's not all that bad.

We have a house we've built up on a peninsula of a fairly small island. The river creeps under the stilts of the house when it's high tide at full moon. The rocks spread around the cove, across the harbor and down to the dock are as tempting as ever. Many times, over several years, I've taken that treacherous path while the others chose the long and safe dirt roads.

Only in the summer does my dad take vacation time. It used to be three to four days a week in the summers, but since the money's gone missing, it's only two days at best.

My mother acts overwhelmed by all the organization that needs her doing, but I think she secretly likes it. For the continuity it interrupts for all of us in some ways, it does provide that feeling of a familiar clean slate.

I wander off with Mandi in tow, up the dirt roads past the houses that haven't been reunited with their people just yet. I like when the area—the point, they call it—is still desolate. The grass is all overgrown, and there's no worry about having to be on good behavior.

In the woods, there are secrets—or at least I've always thought so. There are houses that don't look like anyone's been in them for years, and I like to wonder about them, peering in through the windows. Up here at this time, on the brink of the season, I can wander in my mind and on foot. I've spent so much time in these woods after reading many a mystery book and then psyching myself out. Good times.

This honeymoon stage of being back here in Maine never lasts for too long, so I enjoy what I can. There are fewer fights for a while, as everyone's busy rediscovering the space around them. Angry Brother was even delighted to find that the sea monkeys he'd flushed down the toilet not only survived but grew. He fishes them out of the toilet and sets them back up in a tank in the kitchen because that's not gross or anything.

I call my friend Aaron to tell him I'm here. He's the one who won me my giant white stuffed lion. He lives five minutes up the road on the main part of the island and arrives in a flash. It's always nice to catch up with him. We sit on the floor of my room and embellish stories from the past year.

I ask how his twin brother Chris is, and he brushes it off rather quickly. I've had a crush on Chris since I was eleven, much to Aaron's chagrin. But Chris has only ever seen me as a child or his brother's little friend. The two of them will work at the camp we all met at, and I'll be at the boutique in town.

I love my job at the boutique. I only got the job because both of my older sisters worked there in the past. I think the boss did my dad a favor but is more than happy with how I do. The hardest thing about the job is striking up conversations with strangers. The weirdest part is standing out front with my hand up a duck puppet's ass to encourage intrigue. But I don't mind it. There are worse ways to make money. This guy I know says his dad earns a living shoveling shit at a farm.

At night, I turn off the radio and stare at the stars through the window behind me. I run through the multiple escape routes I've mapped out in my head in case of a break-in.

It's kind of weird not having cameras everywhere in this house. We have a pretty serious alarm system, but we're so isolated before the other houses get filled. Last time it went off it took over an hour for the police to find us. No one has real addresses where we live. We'd all have been dead by the time they arrived if there was any real threat. I've thought about this a lot.

My room is in the most vulnerable, dangerous spot of the house. It's the first room off the front door and protrudes into the driveway, cradled by the front deck. I imagine that if someone broke in by land, I'd be the first to know, and this sets my anxiety on edge.

If the intruders came by sea, my oldest sister's room might be the first explored. We're the only two on the ground floor ever since they built up the second floor. It worries me that she won't be paying attention and give us ample enough warning. When she's up here with us, she often sleeps with her headphones on with loud music blasting.

I have a hard time sleeping at night, so I sleep in on mornings when I can. Among the sounds of the woods and the water, the creaks in the house, who could relax? I hear my parents say how the fresh air makes it so easy for them to get a good sleep, but I think they're all crazy. Besides—if they're not going to worry, it's all left up to me.

LOCAL COLOR

My bosses are an eccentric couple from England and Australia. He looks conservative in buttoned, denim shirts but has a surprisingly twisted sense of humor. I find her less friendly with determined eyes that see past me, always dressed to the nines and with her two-toned hair. She's all business and intimidates me, but I can't help but like her for her individuality.

I don't know how they managed to settle up in Boothbay or how they suffer through the long off-season. I've heard rumors that they have people from all over fly in to stay with them—and that they're swingers. But I just can't picture it. I imagine they have to do something to keep life interesting through the winters though.

I must look different this year because the boys start to take notice. Maybe they can tell that I'm officially sexually active now. I spent my entire last summer in a haze. I probably look a little less deranged now. It's probably the confidence instilled in me from sleeping with Luke.

Oh, Luke... I can't think of Luke. I need to move on.

On my first evening shift, there's this seven-foot-tall man about ten years older than me. He wants to know if I can meet him at the bar when I get off work. I tell him I'm underage. Not only am I underage, but I'm five feet two. I don't know what he's looking for but don't want to be it.

A very sweet older couple comes in, and I help them with the jewelry case. She tries some things on and asks her husband how pretty I am.

He says, "The Koreans are the most beautiful women in the world," impressing me by knowing my brand of Asian.

I look over, apologetically, to his very non-Korean wife as she nods her head, with a smile. And it's all so uncomfortable. They buy a few things and seem tickled to have encountered a real live Asian again.

Being the only slanty-eyed girl up here among all these white tourists makes me a spectacle I guess. It used to be that people would just stare and look curious, but this new thing of being called pretty is strange. I know I can be cute if I try really hard, but I'm not the most beautiful girl by a long shot. I'm just the only one of my kind around here.

As gross as it sounds, I kind of like when it works in my favor. When they're not creepy men or old couples—if they're boys closer to my age—I like the attention. I crave feeling wanted. I can't quite explain it, but it comes from a pretty raw place.

Within my first week of working at the shop, I know it's going to be a good summer. I'm better equipped to make friends and to be around people. Perhaps it's what I needed after this school year: a new chance to come out as the person that I want to be.

The girls who work with me are great. The boss hires only decent-looking young girls, and we all get along fairly well. Three of them are locals and two of us are summer residents, so we get a good mix of people visiting us at work.

I'm quickly invited to a bonfire party at a lighthouse on an island in the harbor. Before leaving Boston, I made myself a fake ID using a photocopier and laminator. There's this one store I've been able to buy from in town. I pick up a big cheap bottle of strawberry Boone's and head for the docks.

I don't know whose boats we take, but a couple of guys were nice enough to pick us up to ride to the party. Half the people are lighting up cigarettes and weed, but I cling to my sweet-tasting cheap wine.

The moon reflects off the ocean, and the wind in my hair makes me feel so grown up. These are the kinds of parties the kids back home only dream of. This is the real deal right here.

When we arrive at the lighthouse, a fire is already roaring. The first crew got it started. Someone sings and plays the guitar. Others sing along, but I'm too shy. I just sip from the bottle and gaze around the circle at everyone who seems so relaxed. No one's trying to out-scream anyone. It's refreshing to see this level of comfort. I'm not used to it. People seem to be content in the *now*, whereas everyone back home's always looking for the next best thing.

Some people run off, giggling together. Others make out steps away from the circle. The guitar's passed around and people take turns leading songs that everyone else seems to know.

A young-looking kid who's probably about my age is peering over at me, trying not to get caught. When I catch him, he asks for my name and where I'm from and doesn't do the annoying double take of where I'm *really* from. I like him for that.

He's a pretty cute kid, but I don't find myself attracted to him. He looks timid, and I'm not into that right now. I need a guy with a little more swagger. I talk to him nicely for a while until I have to pee. Then I use the excuse to move somewhere else and talk to other people when I return.

There's this one guy named Ted, who seems to think he's hot shit. He's scrawny in his ripped jeans and scally cap and slowly sucks on a cigarette. I'm drawn to him instantly and move into his circle to give him a run for his money.

"Is that shit spiked with narcissist-ogens?" I tease.

"Hey, if you've got it, flaunt it," he smirks, lifting his hands to his chest.

"Oh, I've got it," I say, smirking back. "Your number, that is." His ladies look at me with shock for daring to think I can step to him.

"And what number is that," he coaxes.

"I don't know, you look pretty well-seasoned. I'd say about twenty."

"Twenty beers to get this sharp? Shit, that's cheaper than college," he shrugs, but he loves the banter and I know it.

On the boat ride back, girls flock to Ted's side to hear what else he's got to say. He carries on for several nautical miles, only too pleased with himself. I light up a cigarette, acting like I've been doing it my whole life. I turn my head to the sea when I cough and then lean against the side rails, exhaling and blowing smoke in his direction. He keeps talking to the girls hanging on while his cool blue eyes fixate on me.

He's an interesting looking guy with a sharp wit and tongue. He wouldn't normally be my choice, but there's something about him that screams "drunken old poet at seventeen." Naturally, I'm fascinated.

TWO-LETTER WORD

Aaron's got a new cabin at the camp, so I stop in to visit after work one day. It's small and he has to share it, but it's kind of cool that he pretty much has his own place.

His roommate's an older, well-traveled guy who's a little bit off but attentive. He's got Polaroids of topless women by his bed. He claims they're past lovers who are still dear to him but "the road always called him away."

The three of us sit and drink beer while this guy tells us all about the middle states. Like many of the older tourists who work at the camp, he wears who he thinks he is on his lips. It's clear to me within the first five minutes what he wants me to think of him and his life. Nevertheless, he's all right to be around. He's full of stories, be they real or imagined. He's generous with his booze and shows interest in everyone. You can't really argue with that.

Chris, Aaron's twin, pops in. I get up to hug him. He's as cute as ever. I automatically scan Aaron's face and can sense his discomfort, so I cool off and step back. He says he's going to college in Boston, and I can't say I don't like the idea—my long-time crush so close to home; it tugs at a string I'd forgotten was there.

Chris is dating some obnoxious tall blonde from the South who's also working at the camp. She's crass, and she looks like a model. She walks in with her cowboy hat, boots, and slim thighs and asks, "How the fuck 'er y'all?"

I laugh and she says, "What you gigglin' at, shorty?"

"You're funny," I say. "I like your style."

"Meh-el," she says, with two syllables. "That's what they call me when they're bein' nice."

"Millie," I say with a nod. Then I get up and start doing a Milli Vanilli dance, and we all double over in tears. "It's really Millie," I say, regretfully, sitting down.

"Poor thang. Not only are you two feet tall, eh?" she says, holding a can up to me and then swigging back the rest of it.

Chris is such a sweet, laid back guy. When laughing at Mel, I can't help but giggle at the idea of the two of them together. But of course I'm jealous about not being such a vivacious blonde or the girl with his heart.

Stopping in at the camp after work when I'm on day shifts becomes a regular thing. I get to hang out with my best friend *and* my long-time crush. And the others are entertaining.

Late one night when it's just the odd roommate and me, he tells me that he knows about my crush on Chris.

"Aaron won't talk about it," he says, "but Chris said that Aaron forbade it."

"What do you mean?" I ask him, confused.

"Well, Chris says that for some reason Aaron's really protective of you. Said he knew that you liked him all this time but didn't want anything to come between him and his brother."

"Oh," I say, perplexed. "Well, it's not like Aaron has to worry now, anyway. Mel's everything guys ever dream of."

"Some," he says, correcting me. "Not all. She's good-looking, for sure. But she's not really a lady."

"A lady," I repeat with a scoff. "What's a lady worth to anyone these days anyway? Anyone can be a lady. She's hardcore, but I like that she's authentic."

"Is she though?" he says skeptically. "Or maybe she's just taking advantage of being in a new place for a short while, where she can try on whatever she wants?"

I consider what he's said and think about myself and my own personal relaunch. "So what if she is?" I say in her defense. "She's not hurting anyone."

"I prefer a less showy lady," he says. "One that doesn't have to try so hard."

He looks at me with such an odd gaze. I'm a little drunk, so I fall for his smirk. And then he lifts me up off the floor and onto his bed with him. He kisses me dramatically—the way he wants me to believe he's kissed hundreds before, I'm sure. Although he kisses slowly, his hands are much faster than expected—I supposed because of his age, which is—*what?*—I'm not sure.

Before I know it, he's got a condom on and is pushing into me. I clumsily shift up on the bed, pushed away by his force, as his body's much bigger than mine. He moves in about a dozen times before something comes over him and he stops.

"How old did you say you were again?" he asks, breathing into my ear.

"Seventeen," I say, and he starts backing up.

"Whoa, you're too young for me," he says, as if I was the aggressor.

"Hey, this wasn't my idea," I say, making sure we understand each other.

"No, of course not," he says, with a softer, gentler tone. "It was me. I should've thought."

"I'm gonna take off," I say to him, getting myself together. "Tell the others I said bye."

A couple days later at work, I see him lurking around at the shop. One of the girls I work with whispers to me, "See that guy over there? He's checking you out."

"Oh no," I say, biting my lip. "It's this guy who lives at the camp with my friend Aaron."

"He's kinda cute," she says, surveying the scene.

"He's all yours," I say jokingly.

One of the local girls—the petite blonde employee— goes up to him and lays it on pretty thick. She's cute in a homely kind of way and uses old-school country charm to make men feel pampered just by her mere presence. Her flirtations know no bounds though. She treats all men the same. It's just her way. And it works every time. She's told me she's slept with half the men in town, regardless of age, and I believe her.

Just a couple days later, the petite blonde decides she doesn't like him anymore. She says she thought he might have followed her on break to the soda machine. Another girl at the shop said she doesn't trust him either and told her mother we're worried for our safety. I don't know how it all gets so out of hand or if I'm undermining him, but it happens so quickly.

At Aaron's cabin, I slip the older guy a folded letter warning him that the girls are considering a restraining order. I also reiterate that what happened between us was not my doing, and I don't like the way he made me feel. And just like that, two days later Aaron tells me he's skipped town. Makes me wonder about all the girls he says he's left in his wake.

"Maybe he was a serial killer," says Mel, the southern belle.

"I don't think so," I say, "but there was definitely something up with him. How old was he anyway?"

"He wrote twenty-eight on his application," Aaron says.

"Twenty-eight!" I shout. "I slept with a twenty-eight-year-old?"

"You slept with him?" shouts Aaron, completely bewildered.

"Well, no," I say, embarrassed for blurting that out. "The other night I was drunk and he pulled me into his bed. We started doing it, but when he learned how old I was, he stopped."

"He pulled you into his bed?" Aaron exclaims. And all of a sudden he's like my anorexic sister with his echoing.

"Look, it was no big deal," I say, shaking it off. "I shouldn't have said anything. It was a mistake."

"He knew how old you were! I'll kick his ass if he shows his face around here again," says Aaron, all worked up.

My eyes meet Chris's then shift to the floor.

"Your friend's mom was right to call the police," Aaron says. "He's probably a sex offender."

"It really wasn't like that," I say, thinking back on *The Incident*. That was real. "It wasn't violent. Just inappropriate and awkward."

"It's statutory rape!" Aaron says. "Jesus! If he comes near you again, call me."

"Yeah," I promise, wondering what the age of consent is anyway.

Driving home, I feel so mixed about everything. I kind of feel sorry for that guy. I don't think he was all that bad. I'm not sure what happened to cause all the concern so fast. These small-town kids overreact, right? But I don't know. I feel dirty and slightly used. It's barely a fraction of how I felt after *The Incident*, so it's hard for me to put them in the same category.

I never said *no*. I didn't have time to, really. But I never said it.

I think back to *The Incident* and can't recall saying the word *no* then, either. It wasn't framed as a question. There was just the gun and then chaos. I wasn't really there. But perhaps my not saying the word *no* is why he didn't know what he was doing was wrong.

One simple word.

Can one two-letter word really carry such weight?

And now, should I carry the blame?

BREAKING THE BOY

Every few days there's a party around here. So every few days I get pummeled by booze and desperate for quick, emotionless sex. I realize it's become *a thing*, but I allow myself the debauchery. I was such a perfectly obedient kid before, and it didn't do me any good. At least now I get to experience what it's like to have fun. And I'm still always on time for work.

My boss has a new gimmick to get people into the shop. It's a giant bubble maker. I get to stand outside with a wand and a bucket on display making magic happen for the children. Giant bubbles like you've never seen float down past the docks and over the harbor. I mean—you could fit three people in them. Everyone comes to see what other cool things we've got, and I rush in to help them.

I meet people from all over the world but never Asia. Can't say why, but I find myself making fun of my face by trying on circular glasses and telling people in a fake accent,

"I'm Yoko Ono!" This is what happens, I guess, when people start paying attention to the girl who's uncomfortable with her face. But they laugh anyway.

The words of the camp counselor who fled come to mind about taking advantage of being someplace different. Maybe that was why he never stayed put. Perhaps he couldn't maintain whichever character he presented each time. It makes me wonder if this new role of Asian Clown is the persona I want and what kind of pressure it would take to sustain it.

I tell my parents I'll be staying at a friend's house and head up to the party of the night. There's a keg and an abundance of booze, so we just drink whatever's closest to us at the moment. I'm engaged in conversation with a guy with blonde curls who's standing next to the whiskey. So I end up having a few shots in my Coke and lose track of what he's saying.

The next thing I know, I'm being swept into a room by people telling me to put on my pants. I can't say why I had taken them off, but the laughter that ensued had me thinking I should keep emerging sans pants. So I do—until one girl tucks me into bed and brings me a glass of water. Something about the nurturing aspect of this makes me not want to disappoint her, so I let myself fade into the drunken haze.

When I wake and emerge, the party's over. I'm sobering up but by no means sober. The curly blonde guy saunters over with a smirk and latches his face onto mine. We end up in the bathtub, half-naked and half-cocked. And I do mean half-cocked, as he's not fully erect but still insists on trying to have sex.

After he leaves, I decide to stay in the tub. It's kind of comfy, and I like the cool of the porcelain on my cheek. I sleep for as long as I can and am interrupted by the quiet, cute kid from the bonfire party who I'd thought was too timid.

"Oh, I didn't know anyone was in here," he says, maybe half as drunk as I am.

"Do you have to pee?" I slur to him, peering out from behind the shower curtain.

"Um, kinda," he says, looking slightly embarrassed.

"Do you want me to close the curtain or get out?" I say.

"If you wouldn't mind, it'd be easier if you got out for a minute," he says.

I get up and plop myself down outside the door, unintentionally listening to the on and off stream of his pee.

He comes out and sits down next to me.

"Did you have fun?" he asks.

"I think so," I say. "I missed part of it."

"Yeah," he says and starts kissing me.

There's a wire in my head that's been crossed with another. I bring him into the bathroom with me and shut the door.

"Do you have a condom?" I ask.

He nods, "Yeah," and shyly pulls one out.

I undo his pants and pull him out so he can unravel it onto himself. Then I sit on top of him and his innocence as he looks up at me and says, "Are you sure?"

I slide down onto him and say, "Yeah," while I begin. I have control once again. It is mine, and I feel like a warrior.

"What happened?" I say, noticing it softening up.

"I came," he says with an equal look of shame, awe, and

intoxication.

"Oh," I say, getting up to get dressed.

"It was my first time," he says.

"Oh," I say again.

SPIES & SPITE

When I come home after my shift at work the next day, my parents are both in the kitchen. Through the sliding glass doors, I see my mother standing up, watching me get out of the car. As I approach the house, walking across the deck, I notice she's holding something in her hand. And as I open the door, her face reddens as she lifts up one of my notebooks.

"Do you want to explain this?" she says with a snarl.

I just stand there, utterly confused as to what she's doing with my notebook and what she wants me to explain.

"Nothing? You have nothing to say?" she says, louder now.

"It's my notebook?" I say, unsure if that's what she wants but thinking probably not.

She flips a page and starts reading from my notebook, *out loud* and in front of my father, the practice letter that I wrote to Aaron's ex-roommate.

"It wasn't me who climbed into your bed!" she says with effect. "You're the one who pulled me into your bed!"

I have to hand it to her; she could've been quite the stage actor.

"And now you're flirting with girls at work and you might be in trouble! How many of them have you slept with before you asked their age? Did you wait until you were inside of them too?"

I stand there horrified, paralyzed, and humiliated. Everything's so out of context yet way too much truth. But before I can say anything, she flips another page and carries on.

"I'm so glad that you were the one to *take my virginity!*" she shouts.

Oh no. My practice letter to Luke.

"You were the perfect guy for the job!" she says even louder.

"That's my *private book*!" I say to her, at last. "You have no right to spy!"

"Spy?" she says, as if it's a ridiculous word. "I have no right to spy? We're concerned!"

"Well—it's a little late for that!" I shout back.

"I can't believe you, Millie!" she says and adds a look of disgust. "I never would have expected this—especially not from *you!*"

My dad pipes up, loudly, with, "Why do you have to have a guy?"

And that's it. I turn on my heel and walk into my room, slamming the door behind me. I open it up and slam it three more times and then fall face down onto the bed.

How dare she? Has she ever stopped spying on me? Why am I not entitled to one little piece of privacy?

And what did she mean by "especially not from me"? Because I was raped or because I'm so ugly?

How much worse could my life possibly get?

Why am I at fault for dealing with my shit my own way? What other way was I supposed to do it? She doesn't know what it's been like for me. How dare she shout out my most private thoughts like that—so carelessly!

This is not love. This is not family. This is not how shit gets dealt with. It's not fair for her to do this to me when she was never there when I needed her most.

I keep shouting in my head all the things that I wish I had the courage or strength to go out and shout to her face. My heart's in total shock from the hatred I felt radiating from her and the look of resentment and disgust from my father.

Why do I have to have a guy, Dad?

The words echo in my head as I think them so loudly.

I don't know! I just do! But you don't understand those letters. Neither of you ever understood anything about me!

I clench my teeth and all of my muscles as tightly as I can to refrain from crying. I hate to cry. Crying is nothing but a cheap ploy for attention. If I really wanted attention from them, I'd kill myself, finally, after a decade of lies.

I doubt they'd even miss me. Sure—they'd tell everyone how much they loved me, but all they care about is what everyone else thinks. If I do kill myself someday, they'll be more upset that everyone will think they failed as parents than by my actual death.

I live partly out of spite. They don't deserve the false pity.

HUMAN COMPLICATIONS

Turning down parties sucks dick and telling people why sucks even bigger dick. I'm seventeen fucking years old. Pretty soon I'll be free to leave the house and do whatever the fuck I want. I'll get a year-round job and an apartment. Maybe I'll take a couple of the cats and a dog.

"Your mom spies on your diaries?" asks one of the girls at work.

"You have no idea," I tell her. "She's been spying on them since I was seven. Ten years. Ten fucking years of spying on my life. I hope it's entertaining!"

"That's crazy," she says. "My mom and I have a pact to never break each other's trust."

"Lucky for you," I tell her. "Maybe that's the beauty of having only one sister. You can actually care about each other's feelings rather than be so overwhelmed that no-body's really matter."

"Whoa, that blows," she says, sympathizing with me. "I

guess I have it pretty good."

I want to pick up something and throw it at her, but it's not her fault.

"I'm glad that things are normal for you," I say instead, biting my tongue.

"Hey, I didn't say normal," she says with a giggle. "I hear my mom and my step-dad having sex every night. It's embarrassing. And then she comes into my room in a frenzy to bum cigarettes off me."

"Ew," I cringe.

"Yeah," she says and goes about straightening out the merch in the shop.

"So what did she spy on when you were seven?" she asks, dusting glass countertops. "That you wanted the pink dolly dress instead of the purple one?"

"Yeah, right," I say, giggling. "More like how I wanted to kill myself."

"What?" she nearly screams between a half-smile.

"Oh yeah, I wanted to kill myself at seven. Don't know why. But she did the same thing to me back then. Read everything out loud to me while I sat there horrified. I don't know why she thinks that's a good approach," I say, contemplating and shaking my head.

"So what happened? I mean, I can see you didn't kill yourself," she laughs. "But what did she do?"

"We tore it up and flushed it all down the toilet and pretended like it never happened," I recall. "I mean, I know she kept spying. They've got this thing about depriving us of privacy. My house back home is equipped with surveillance cameras and intercoms all through the house."

"Are you shitting me?" she says with disbelief. "Even

your bedrooms?"

"Yep. I shit you not," I say, cleaning glass cabinets.

"What—are they paranoid?" she asks.

"Maybe," I say, thinking about it. "I don't know. My mom says my dad just really likes gadgets. He has to have the first of everything—the first VCR, camcorder, whatever."

"Hmmm," she considers, "sounds pretty fucked up."

"Perhaps it is," I say. "I have no perspective when it comes to them anymore."

One of our new friends dances in, high off her tits, telling us about the next party.

"Later tonight," she sings, "I hear something's going on at Margie's place."

"I'm in!" says my coworker.

"I'm out," I pout. "Don't ask why because the answer's: life sucks."

Hippy girl shrugs at my coworker, and she shrugs back. Then the two of them go on about which level of awesomeness will hit while I organize sweaters in the next room.

I listen to music on my Walkman in bed while I gaze up at my old bookshelf. I used to love to read so much. Judy Blume and Beverly Cleary sure promised a life that I never quite found. And all my *Sweet Valley* series... Ugh. Those were the days, imagining I could not only be a blonde, blue-eyed beauty but a *twin* rather than an Asian island out here on my own. To have someone who looked just like me to play tricks on people with, instead of this torture, would be nothing short of magic.

Some people must just love their lives. It's so easy for them—the beautiful and the rich. You probably only need to be one to have the other, so all it takes is just beautiful *or* rich. I live in two houses, which makes it appear as if I were rich, but it's only a big façade. I also live in one body but have two lives.

Angry Brother opens my door and shouts, "Don't pick up the phone when it rings! Dad's expecting a fax, fuckhead!" and slams the door.

Of course. My dad drives all the way up here just to sit by the fax machine for two days and bitch to my mother about business and the fact that he can't find more money that's gone missing. It's more peaceful when he's gone, honestly. It's not like he ever smiles or gets us excited by announcing we're going out on the boat anymore. The boat bobs by the buoy a couple hundred feet from the kitchen, feeling just as neglected as the rest of us.

I get up out of bed to go search for a cat. I grab the first one I can find and take him back to bed.

Snuggling with Maggie always makes me feel better. He's always so thankful for the human touch. His long dark fur looks so fancy, like a handsome little man who should wear a bowtie and sit at the head of a long table. I treat him as if he's a prince. And he loves me right back with his purrs and his paws.

If love can really be this simple, why do humans overcomplicate things?

NO HOUDINI

It's just another ordinary, boring night until I hear my father screaming my name.

"Millie, get out here now!" he demands with a bellow.

"All right, I'm coming!" I shout back furiously. Man, I've always gotta drop everything I'm doing as soon as I hear them call.

I open the door and can't see anyone right away, so I yell, "Okay, I'm here!"

"Come upstairs! We need your help!" he shouts.

I look up and see most of the family gathered in the little landing on top of the stairs.

"What are you *dorks* doing?" I say.

"Just shut up and get up here, okay?" Dad yells.

Moping, I thump up the stairs, not understanding why everything always has to be such a big production in this family. The old "how many clowns does it take to screw in a light bulb" joke comes to mind, but I keep it to myself.

"Mandi locked herself in," Dad says, when I arrive.

I start to laugh. *Oh, that dog!* But Dad's not the least bit amused.

"We've been trying for twenty minutes to get her out. The hinges are on the inside and the lock's not budging," he says.

"Well, maybe you shouldn't be allowed a lock either—like the rest of us," I say.

"I don't need your smart mouth right now," he says.

"What do you want me to do?" I huff.

"I need you to go around and climb up the side of the house. Your mother thinks the window's open," he says. "You can climb through it and unlock the door."

"Are you serious?" I say. "Nobody else can do this?"

I guess I'm the only expendable of the bunch, not being their real kid.

"You're the only one strong enough to do it," he says.

"Oh my God," I sigh with an eye roll. "Fine. Whatever. Who's gonna help?"

Angry Brother and I go around the house to our little beachfront. We get the small ladder out from under the deck. It's not long enough to reach the window, so we prop it up against the roof over the kitchen. I'll have to pull myself across and over.

"Hold it steady, and don't mess around," I say to him.

I climb up the ladder to the inclined roof and steady myself so not to fall back. Holding on to some shingles, I inch my way across the two-inch roofing that hangs a few feet below my parents' bathroom window. I try to nudge the window with my hand but it's locked.

"Don't fall, jackass," says my brother.

"Gee thanks," I mumble, holding on to the window frames.

I stretch my body as far as I can and reach over to the open window. I push the screen with my fingers and it slides a little.

"Are you in, Millie?" I hear my dad scream from inside the house and the other side of the door.

"Not yet! Don't mess me up!" I shout, as my foot slips a little off the shingle.

I see Mandi sitting, facing the door. She turns her head around when she hears me and starts wagging her tail.

"I'm coming to get you," I sing to her in a little voice.

I'm not as strong as I used to be since I quit gymnastics and stopped working out as often as I did. My arms shake a bit while I try to pull my own weight through the window to somersault in onto the floor. But when I do, there's a *boom*, and Mandi's tongue starts to lick my face and neck all over.

"Ahhh! You're tickling me!" I yell, laughing. "Mandi!" I giggle, getting up to pat her head and open the door.

"Mandi!" everyone says, patting her all over. "You're too damned smart! How did you lock yourself in?"

My dad takes a look at the door and says, "She must've turned the knob and leaned on it here so that it rotated and locked."

But nobody pays attention to him. They didn't really want to know how she did it. I think my dad's the one person in the world who's more awkward than me.

I walk down the stairs saying, "You're welcome for coming to the rescue," to no one.

When I go to my room to sleep, Mandi nudges the door open behind me, so I shut it behind her.

"No locks on this door," I tell her, tickling behind her ears as she pants at me.

She climbs up and sits on my stomach.

"Ugh!" I moan as she stands up and repositions herself in a crescent moon.

IT'S NOT ME, IT'S YOU

"It has to be her," my mother shouts at my dad. "There's no other way to explain it."

My father stares out toward his boat, which hasn't gotten any use since the day it came out of the marina.

"Just listen to me," she says, pleading her case. "All of her bookkeeping is gibberish. I've been trying to figure it out and it's impossible. She says it all makes sense to her, but when I try to get her to explain it to me, she can't!"

I duck out of the house without them noticing. The upside of the continued saga of missing money is that they've forgotten I'm supposed to be grounded.

These two guys we know rent a small house on the hill looking over the center of town. We sit on the roof, sipping out of plastic cups and listening to the radio from another guy's convertible.

"Pearl Jam or Nirvana," someone poses.

"Ooh, that's a tough one," says another. "They both have

their merits."

This is the kind of argument I'd much rather hear.

I breathe in the crisp ocean air and lean back a little, happy to be free. I take a sip of my mystery beer—which is probably composed of at least two mixed as one—and glance around at these people I now call friends.

As my eyes move from hippy girl to grunge boy to goth, I smile at the collection of people I get to spend time with. Surely they're all real friends, as they spend the rest of their year together. They build histories and can talk about things that happened way back when they were five. It's nice to be immersed in a group of people who commit to at least being who they think they are in the moment. Nobody's too cool for anything or anybody.

Just as I'm lost in my feelings of gratitude, they all disappear from the roof to smoke a bowl. I stand up and walk across the roof to sit out on the deck below. When I'm three-quarters of the way there, I see my mother peering up at me while she's driving through town.

Shit. I hope she didn't see my face.

When my friends are all nice and stoned, we sit in a large circle on the floor of the living room. Phil positions himself in the middle, strumming on his guitar, and bellows deeply with intense emotion. He's so confident in himself with his eyes closed. All of ours are on him as he sings about love lost.

"Torn... like an old... dollar bill..."

I don't know what that's like—to be anything like that. When I used to sing, it was full of pretense and nerves. Sure, I wrote my own songs and played all the music, but I didn't own my voice or the feeling behind it.

I close my eyes and listen to Phil. It's so beautiful being in the presence of a man with so much controlled raw emotion. I forget for a moment the way he talks about some of my friends and probably me when I turn my back. In this moment, he's everything that I wish I could be.

More and more beer is consumed from the lack of getting high, and I realize I'm not on anyone's level. When they're stoned, I feel miles away—even when I'm drunk. I'm suddenly curious about weed but not sure if I want to go there just yet. I just want to connect.

In the doorway I see a familiar shape of a guy. He gesticulates fancifully with a cigarette in his hand. I hear his voice, and I know instantly that it's Ted, the drunken poet I met back on the island. He sees me out of the corner of his eye but keeps talking to his friend as if not at all distracted.

Phil hands me a cigarette. I light it up, despite the fact that I haven't smoked since that first time on the boat across from Ted. I talk to Phil and his friend about music and how someday I'd like to learn the guitar.

Phil's friend seems to like me maybe a little too much, meaning that the feelings are not reciprocated. He follows me around, asking weird questions.

"Hey Millie, is it fun being an Asian goddess?" And "Hey Millie, did you make that thing in your hair?"

Forty-five minutes to an hour later, Ted randomly bumps into me just a little too slickly. He says, "Hey, you're that wise ass from the bonfire party."

"Am I?" I say with a smile. "I thought that was you."

"Want one?" he says, holding out a pack of Camels. I take one and hold it out for him to light.

"Thanks, man," I say, trying to play it cool.

"You from Portland?" he asks.

"Boston," I tell him.

"Not a bad little city," he says, lighting his cig.

"Where are you from?" I say, puffing coolly beside him.

"I'm from the seed of my alcoholic dad and the womb of my abusive mother," he says casually, and I suspect it's the truth.

"No shit," I say.

"I assure you, it's actually quite shitty," he says, exhaling.

I sip my beer, looking around at all the happily faded people.

"What brings you down here?" he says.

"My spy of a mother and my paranoid father," I say.

"No shit," he laughs.

"I assure you, it's also quite shitty," I say, grinning.

Ted and I find a spot outside on the deck. We chain smoke and drink beer while I tell him about my house in Boston. He's interested in digging deep into the psychology of my parents, and although it's uncomfortable, it's nice to have someone offer his insights for once.

"That's a lot of kids, man," he sighs. "That's the problem with the mentality that more is always more. We live in a world where we compete for insanity and where insanity is actually practiced more than organized religion—which is insanity in itself too. People letting others tell them how to live because they're too cowardly to make their own rules and beliefs. It's madness."

He likes to hear himself talk, but I kind of do too.

Later on when everyone's pretty far gone, we sneak off to a vacant room. He wants to see me completely naked and says he likes girls with muscle. In fact, he says I should try to build up more.

"I don't want to look like a man," I say, feeling his smooth chest.

"You could never," he says, sliding his hands across my bare skin.

I can see him faintly, from the street lights filtering in through the cracks of the curtains. He's lean and firm and surprisingly hairless. I don't comment on it though.

He gives me his dog tags and tells me to keep them.

"Really?" I say, surprised. "Aren't they kind of important?"

"Are you saying you're not also important?" he says.

We start to have sex, but the condom gets in the way. I then notice he's not fully erect.

Another one, I sigh to myself.

"I take medication for other shit," he says, still trying.

It lasts for only about a minute at a time. I pretend to enjoy it more than I do because I want to enjoy it more than I am. Somehow I think that will help but it doesn't.

I tell him that it's okay as we dress, and he starts acting like it's my fault.

"You should carry around a lubricant," he says. "You're like sandpaper."

"What?" I say, confused and a wee bit insulted.

"I can't come when a girl is like sandpaper," he says.

"Oh," I say, leaving it at that.

HIGHS & LOWS

Somehow, despite my resurgence of partying, I'm selling more at the boutique. My bosses are so happy with the big sales I've helped make that they give me a couple hundred dollars extra this week. It seems I don't really need sleep as much as I need freedom.

This girl we party with stops by with a few people one night when we're getting ready to close. A surfer-looking dude she's with says he's having some people over if we want in. We kick them out, vacuum up, and do the till. Within twenty minutes, we're pulling into his driveway.

Surfer Dude carries a giant hookah into the living room while everyone gasps with delight. I tell them I think I'm ready to try smoking weed, and they tell me I'm doing it Cadillac-style. Radiohead's *Creep*, the unedited version, is blaring loudly through the speakers. We all sit in a circle taking turns on the hookah's arms, giving ourselves to the moment.

After a couple of hits, I lean back and fall over. I fumble into a nice chair and melt into it. And when the pedal kicks on and the chorus kicks in, it's like the sound lifts me up and smashes me against the wall in the most pleasant way.

"How do you like it, Millie?" someone asks from across the room.

I just smile.

A friend drives my car to my place while another drives me home. At the edge of the driveway, they ask if they think I can successfully pull in and stop the car without crashing. I think I can, and with much luck I do. They drive off quietly, and I sneak my way into bed.

The room is spinning in a nice slow fashion. I notice Mandi's on the floor by the bed. She must've been waiting for me to get home.

"You're like my old lady now, huh?" I say, patting her head as her tail thumps the floor.

I put in a mix tape that Surfer Dude gave me and let the music from my headphones spiral through my ears. The world is magical, and I can't understand why people say that pot's a bad thing to do.

I think about my oldest sister and all of her bones. I wonder how she's doing down in Boston this week. I think about the angry brother and why he does what he does, and why my sister did what she did to get skinny—each side, polar opposite extremes.

There's a soft spot that gets nudged when I think of my parents and how they can't seem to get a grip on anything these days. I wonder if they'll be able to keep it together and whether my skinny sister got skinny and my fat brother got fat as a subconscious means for attention. I really don't fault my parents because as much as we hate each other most of the time, I do think they mean well. They've just overextended themselves so much that it's impossible to keep track of everybody and everything. That, and they always think they're right.

My mother's parents have a tiny little cottage across the driveway from us. They've been traveling in Nova Scotia. The next morning I hear their car pull into the white stone driveway. I look up and out the window to see Missy—the little white terrier—wag her tail nearly straight off her.

Nana's the only one who's good with her. She's a peculiar dog. She can be good with me too, but she's much more complicated than Mandi. Nana seems to understand her. Nana understands everybody.

When Papa gets out of the car, my younger sister runs, gushing into his arms while he cackles with joy. She's always been his little angel. I don't think she could be loved more, to be honest. He doesn't even see her bratty side. They say he's blinded by her looking exactly like Mom used to.

I don't get along with Papa so much. We pretend to like each other sometimes, but he doesn't hide his feelings about me. It still burns when he makes comments and favors my younger sister, but at least I have Nana.

Nana thinks I could be a concert pianist someday if I ever decide to play again. I haven't touched it since *The Incident*, but she doesn't know about that. She just thinks that I got bored. So she says I can be a writer or an artist or whatever I want because I'm beautiful, talented, and special.

Nana doesn't know shit about me or my life, but she loves me with intention, and I need it like water and light.

Someday I'd like to look at my Nana without having to

protect her from my secrets. Maybe then, if she doesn't disown me, I'll experience my first instance of true unconditional love.

"Where do you want to go to college," she asks, as we walk around purposefully stepping on potentially poisonous mushrooms. We throw them into a bag so the dogs won't eat them.

"I don't know," I tell her honestly. "I don't think that I want to." But really, I don't want to bring it up for my parents to fight more about money.

"Well, I guess you don't have to," she says. "But you're smart enough to go if you change your mind."

"I haven't been doing well in school these past couple of years," I say, omitting the reason why.

"Just keep trying, sweetie. I know someday you'll make us all proud. We're proud of you now, but you know what your Nana's saying."

And I do.

I don't tell her it's too late to make her proud though. I can't say that we'll ever share that moment where she beams down at me, and I beam back at her, filled with a deep sense of accomplishment and pride.

"Sometimes things happen in life that we never plan," she says. "You know, we thought we were all set with our house before the fire. But I guess that just wasn't meant to be. God's got other plans for us sometimes."

I don't tell her that I don't believe in God or things being meant to be because that would make a cruel God.

"Yeah," I say, meekly, instead.

"You'll find your way. I have every confidence in that. Ever since the day you wrote that poem—that song—I knew you would do great things with your life," she says.

I want to cry. Not because that song was about how I wasn't pretty at age seven. And not because I've already fucked everything up. I want to cry because it's so hard for me to hear that she still somehow believes in me, that someone in this world really does.

WHEN IT ALL ENDS IN TEARS

I've been thinking about the kid whose virginity I took cheaply in the bathroom that night. I wish he'd told me it was his first time before it all happened. In the state of mind I was in, maybe it wouldn't have made a difference. But somehow I feel as if I've robbed him of something. I felt a surge of power in the moment, not knowing what I was doing, and that makes me feel all the worse. I know it's not the same thing, but I can't help but wonder if I'm no better than my rapist.

When I'm sober and bored in between customers at work, I can see all the ways I'm doing wrong. There's a part of me who so badly wants to rewind, rewind to a time when this life and this world didn't seem so sickening to me. Yet there's a part of me now that needs this life—everything about it, ugly moments and all.

Like my brother, I'm angry. I want something so impossible right now that I keep feeding myself its opposite because I know that I can. It doesn't matter if it takes me further and further from where I want to be. If anything, it perpetuates feeling justified in my actions.

Or maybe like my sister, I'm so hungry for positive attention that I've starved myself of the good things that warranted it. I don't make music anymore. I don't draw. I don't write. I'm shedding myself of the only things in life that ever gave me pure enjoyment.

Maybe my polar opposite siblings are more alike than they think, and that's why they hate each other so much. Maybe my brother can see the weakness in me, and that's why he tries to pummel it out of me.

Maybe we're all so fucked up from disappointment.

Or maybe we're all just spoiled brats.

We have two roofs when so many have none. We have plenty to eat and to look down upon. God damn us for our privilege—the one thing that keeps our problems from being legit.

I was raped. And I know that in some places, there are children being raped several times a day. At least I wasn't killed, right? I should be so thankful to be alive and so thankful to live with the guilt.

Just like I should be thankful that my parents rescued me from the terrible life I'd have had in Korea since my birth parents threw me away. Had I not been adopted, I may not have lived this long. Then again, I may not have been raped. Which is worse? Which should I be more thankful for?

You know, pity parties are boring. This is why I go out

and get loaded.

We go to Surfer Dude's house again. We bring booze, and he brings out the hookah. I love the way that it isolates the moment. Even moments have moments that we'd otherwise miss—pockets you can drop yourself into, slides to swirl down. It's like a fun house in your own mind.

One of my friends tells me that Surfer Dude wants me to stay over. I like his vibe and decide that I will. We make out passionately. Well, he makes out with me, and I follow his lead. My body doesn't even feel real.

He lays me back on this oversized chair in the living room and makes me feel like nothing I've ever felt before. I can't believe my body is capable of feeling the way it does; it's that good. It's a never-ending series of surprises.

The next morning when he leaves for work, he tells me to stay as long as I'd like. I look around his place, but there's nothing that really interests me about him except his presence.

Nonetheless, it becomes a regular thing that we do—getting high and having earth-shattering, emotionless sex. We party with friends, so we share a few jokes. Nothing rivals or supports the physicality of us though.

Ted shows up at a bar we're all at. He plays it cool, as he always does. He sits a few stools over from me, alternating beer and cigarette. And so begins the rivalry of Ted and Surfer Dude.

Surfer Dude says I should stay away from Ted because he's been calling me a loose woman. Ted says Surfer Dude's full of shit and besides, he's as dumb as the cum from his father. All this male drama makes my head spin, and I just wish I could pair the conversations with Ted and the sex with Surfer Dude. Instead, I deal with them and their deficiencies for a few weeks before I stop seeing them both.

I hear Surfer Dude's sleeping with this other girl I've met a few times. She's beautiful with long curly hair and blue eyes. And as much as I never wanted much with him, this somehow enrages a part of me. It feels like rejection—even though I'd already decided I didn't want to be with him.

I find myself doing weird things. A couple of times I go to his house when I know he won't be there. I look around, sniff his pillows, and sit in the chair we always did it in. All of a sudden he's interesting to me—in my mind, at least. It's fucked up. I know.

I've been hanging around with this other crew now. They're friends with another coworker. There's this kid Jared who I remember from years back. He used to flirt with me at the movie theater before I knew anyone in town. It was always embarrassing, though, because I was with Angry Brother, and I think people assumed we were on a date. I mean—they'd never guess we were siblings.

Jared and his friends are the smart kids who look like wasters. With long hair, worn jeans, and ripped flannels, you'd never suspect what comes out of their mouths. And I think they do that on purpose. They want you to write them off just so they can step up with a monologue about why society's shit, citing three or four sources, leaving you dumbfounded.

I show up at Jared's after he calls me over. He greets me with kisses and bravado. There's a lilt in his speech and a snap in his moves. He's so charming and certain about what he's setting out to do. It's really hot. He slowly dances as he undresses us both, and the sex feels pretty damned good. Not as good as with Surfer Dude, but good.

And then he comes.

I look at him; he buries his face and starts crying. He's bawling so hard that he shouts "Go!"

So I dress as quickly as I can, offering rejected consolation. When I realize that I can't get through to him, I go, swiftly closing the door behind me.

I sleep with him again because I want to know if it's a thing. It's an exact reenactment. He starts off so smooth, then it all ends in tears. I try to stay with him, patting his shoulder or knee, but he shoves me off. So I go again.

I come back a couple more times and keep leaving just as soon as he's done. He doesn't want to talk about it. And when we're all together with friends, he acts like nothing ever happened.

I think about Jared's unspoken hurt.

Was it his mother? Father? An aunt? A situation like mine?

I wish he'd open up to me. Maybe then I could open up to him.

There's a part of me that wants to kiss away his tears, tell him I understand. I never thought he'd be so broken inside. No one would ever guess.

I wonder if I'm as good as he is at pretending—or maybe better since I never cry.

CAN'T MEASURE CRAZY

The Summer of Sex goes by all too fast. Every person I've slept with is like an unfinished song: some of them had promise, but most of them barely captured a moment. They were gratuitous fun for the lack of true creative inspiration. In the same way no one ever really needs dessert, I didn't need them either. Yet the craving for the taste always won.

I make the rounds to say goodbye to everybody and wish them a good year. We reminisce on the laughs that we've shared, the debauchery, and give back each other's clothes. We hug and with each clumsy embrace, it seems as though I've spent my whole life saying goodbye. My lack of permanence is highlighted, and I wish that it weren't.

Packed up with no space to spare, our convoy winds its sad way back home from summer. We leave quieter than how we arrived, with less spirit and determination. And since my car is so packed, I drive alone.

School will start up again. Just the thought of unpacking is enough to make me want to drive off a bridge, but I wouldn't want to deal with the fallout of a mere handicap if I annoyingly survived.

Arriving back home doesn't share the same nostalgia as driving up to our summer house. We haven't been gone long enough, and the mysteries aren't nearly as enticing. I put all my stuff away immediately so that I can relax and feel some sense of stillness.

I lean back under my giant white lion and reflect on all that I'll miss: crashing into the ocean at night, chasing boys in cars, skinny dipping, getting high atop rocks and rooftops, and drinking on unpoliced islands sure beats the fuck out of going back to school. This town full of fancy cars, gold chains, and bad accents has got nothing on summers in Maine. People here have too much pride in what they have on the outside, but most of them don't have any real soul.

I don't want to think of Luke but I do. My eyes squeeze tightly to block out visions of girls he's probably been with. But who am I to be jealous? If he only knew his little virgin now and of all the guys who didn't have to work as hard as he did.

Watching the dogs and cats reacquaint themselves with the house cheers me up a bit. Their noses check to make sure all their favorite places are still where they should be. They inspect everything until they're satisfied and take turns hanging out in the VIP spots. Freddie is particularly fond of sitting in the bay window in the living room that overlooks the street. I like to imagine him as Pepé le Pew scanning the street for his next potential sweetheart.

My oldest sister comes up the stairs in an olive-colored

string bikini. There are too many bones to count, but supposedly she's doing better. I don't dare tell her that, though, because when anyone says "you look good," she takes that to mean she's getting fat.

I don't know what she uses to gauge her thinness, her beauty, or self-worth anymore. The scale was her friend-turned-enemy because of the rare occasion of water weight or, God forbid, muscle. I think she's so used to everything lying to her—the scale, the mirror, mean kids—that she trusts nothing and nobody. Can't say that I blame her. But still, it's hard to look at no matter how badly she wants us to see her.

"Will you weigh yourself for me, Millie?" she asks.

Not this again.

"I don't feel like it," I say, hating when she does this.

"I just need to see if the scale is right," she says.

"I don't even know how much I weigh," I tell her. "How will I know if it's right?"

Then she raises her voice to a screech, "Can you just do this for me, Millie? It's all I'm asking!"

My face freezes, wide-eyed. Reluctantly, I go into the bathroom with her in tow. I take off my shoes and stand on the guilty gray scale while she inspects it from all angles.

"One twenty-two? That can't be right," she says.

"Well, it probably is," I tell her.

"But you look smaller than that. It must be off," she insists.

"I've always weighed more than what people expect. Ever since I was little at the doctor's," I say. "Maybe I'm just heavier than I look."

"Nonsense," she says, shaking her head. "It's at least

five pounds off, maybe ten."

I just shrug and let her do her deductions in her head.

Maybe Ted was right in that the greater population of the world really is insane. Most of my family is, anyway. Myself included.

Later at night, when everyone's engrossed in their own TVs, I take the little stash my Maine friends gave me into the bathroom and lock the door. I sit on the blue and white tiles with a Ouija board, deseeding and destemming the weed from the baggie. It's a painstaking process, but it must be done. I flush all the unwanted little bits down the toilet a few times since they're stubborn little floaters.

I've given up trying to roll joints. Even with the fancy roller I got, I suck. I found a nice little pipe at a store that sells incense and beads. It's an ugly little clay and metal thing, but it does the trick. I hide the Ouija board in one of the bottom cabinets that people throw junk in.

With everyone asleep, I sit on the edge of my bed and crack open the window. I take a few deep inhales and let the magical smoke infiltrate my lungs. I exhale out to the dark empty streets lit by the occasional streetlight, but there's nothing to see. Nobody lives around here anymore. They sleep, and they do what they've got to do.

I hide my pipe and my weed in a little tin box that was given to me when I was a kid. It's filled with embroidery string, beads and buttons, fishing wire, sewing needles and shit. I figure it's safe in there. I go back to my window and gaze out at the nothingness, the hazy sky with few stars. I think of all the me's I have been.

I don't even know who I was born as or born to, but I know I was left with no note. I started out as a baby without a family, maybe an orphan but probably not. If I was an orphan, it would mean both my parents were dead. Yet people have always said that my mother was probably young and couldn't keep me. So that would just mean unwanted.

Can't say where I was between then and the six months it took to be flown into Boston. But at that point I became Millie Vaniti, despite who I once was or may have been. I became the third daughter to an Irish Italian—but mostly Italian—American family. Just like that, I had a new identity. I was supposedly saved from the unknown. It sounds like the Korean-American Orphan Protection Program. Heh.

From then on, I became Grateful Daughter, a.k.a. The Lucky One. I went from having nobody to two parents and two sisters. I became part of Christmas card pictures and regular American life. I got to watch cartoons, TV shows, and movies. I got all my own toys. Everything they gave me I was, in return, to be thankful for and be the daughter they wanted.

I tried really hard to be the daughter they wanted. Everyone always had such hope for me. With nobody's genes, I had surprise talents that weren't gifts from them. They were in awe over my need to write stories, draw pictures, and play the piano. I was an alien child with nothing but hope.

I didn't ask for much, but what I wanted, they gave. In return I studied hard in school and did my chores. I was always reminded of how lucky I was to be in school here in America—not by my family so much as their friends and other relatives. I was so lucky—so, so very lucky for all the opportunities I had.

And then I fucked it all up.

I guess I wasn't grateful enough because I wanted to explore life beyond my family's wishes. I wanted to see the city beyond the suburbs and meet black kids, Hispanic kids, and the occasional Asian kid. I took comfort in knowing people outside of our squeaky clean bubble, how they lived and what they wanted out of life.

I stuck a pin in the bubble, and it popped in my face.

I never allowed myself to be the rape victim. Call it stubbornness, but I call it pride. I refuse to be defined by such ugliness—in the way that no one likes me to say I was abandoned but prefer the word saved.

I don't even want to be a rape survivor. Just take that word out of my descriptor now, please, because if you call me by that name, I will not stand.

Who I was is not who I am, and nobody has ever been able to aptly describe who I should be.

Am I Korean? No. I don't speak the language or know anything about Korea except for where it is on the map.

Am I American? No, because people here call me Chinese.

Am I Korean-American? Not really, because my family didn't immigrate from Korea.

My family smiles and says with all certainty that I'm one of them, but everyone else can see that I'm not. What you want is not always so. I don't think, for all of their efforts combined, that they can acknowledge that without feeling some deep regret and denial.

I was lying to myself and to Luke when I said I was a virgin. A virgin wouldn't know what I'd known by the first time we gave it a try. A virgin probably wouldn't have seen other dicks or have been forced to do anything with them.

Afraid to be the victim, I became the slut. I slept with

guys just to feel I wasn't broken and to trick myself into believing that I had control. And I'll probably do it again and as often as I can with whoever fits the bill.

This is just who I am now. Maybe I'm crazy, but I don't know who else I could be.

MONTREAL IS FOR LOVERS

School sucks. It's the same two-hundred-odd people who couldn't give a shit about me. I play nice, though, and ask about their summers just to brag about the epic one I had. It's the first time I'm not envious of their trips to the beach and the bonding they've done without me.

Senior year, eh? At least this whole thing's almost over. If I'm lucky, I'll graduate somewhere in the middle of the class. I know I could've done better if circumstances were different, but if I'm to lose sleep over anything, it won't be that.

Sometimes I call the boys up in Maine and have nothing to say. I just want the connection. I've called Jared—the one who cries after sex—a few times. One time he put me on hold and never picked the phone back up. In the background I could hear other people playing cards with him and the occasional question of, *Is she still there?* I should've hung up, but I just sat on the phone like a moron wondering what else they'd say. It was a pretty ballsy move on his part, given the things I could say if I were that mean a girl.

Angry Brother comes into my room with one of Mom's high-heeled shoes. He throws it at me, and the heel digs into the middle of my chest so hard that I fall to the floor.

I yell, "You... fat... jerk!"

And just like that, I said it. He finally broke me. I wonder if he's happy now.

There are so many things I could say to so many people if I wanted to be like that. I try not to hurt anyone. Truly, I do. I know what it's like to be made fun of for something you can't help. It's such a vulnerable feeling of exposure to be called something you're not proud of but can't help.

My words hurt me more than they hurt him, I bet. He made me just as bad as the others.

The bruise on my sternum grows into a welt. I put a bag of frozen corn over it, and Mandi lays by my side occasionally licking it. I can't tell if she's tending to me or is hoping for scraps. I don't mind either way. It's just nice to feel the warmth of her up against me.

Someday I'll get out of this house and the fuck out of this town. I don't know where I'll go, but I'll go, and I'll never look back. Maybe I'll steal Mandi, and the two of us will find a cute little place to live in peace.

I can't count how many times I've thrown all my prized possessions into black trash bags with the threat of going somewhere and never coming back. I've thought really hard about who could come take me away from this mess, but the truth is, there's no one.

I don't think I even wanted to leave as much as I wanted them to make me want to stay. But they never tried. They just yelled and slammed the door, laughing behind my back.

Kellie and Samantha call me on three-way. They want to know what I think about taking the senior trip to Montréal in March.

"Hey, it's on the weekend of my birthday," I say. "I'll be turning eighteen, so I can drink."

"I'll be eighteen already," says Kellie. "We'll all be able to drink!"

"Sucks that it's with all the kids at school though," I say. "Screw it. I'm in. I still have money left from the summer."

"Best trip everrrrrr," sings Samantha.

Finally, something new to look forward to. I get my parents to sign the permission slip for the tour company and tell them I won't need any of their money.

In the meantime, Luke never calls, and I never call him.

It turns out that the Holiday Inn is like a Holiday Inn anywhere. I don't know what I was expecting—except maybe a little local flavor. Something better than green carpets and tacky bedspreads.

We get dressed to the nines and head down Ste-Catherine Street where all the action's supposed to be. The girls pull me into a dimly lit male strip club and it's amazingly cheesy. Sculpted shiny men dance around in G-strings, and the first thing I notice is that none of them are erect.

I ask a guy, "How come none of you are hard? Don't we turn you guys on?"

He tells me it's against regulation to get hard. They have

to jack-off before performing so they don't get fined, he says. I ask him what's the point, and he just walks away.

Kellie decides to order me a private dance by some guy who is totally not my type. None of them look like my type, but I go along with it since they're adamant that I do. He does his thing, and it's extremely awkward and pointless. I think he notes my discomfort and starts talking to me.

"Where are you from?" he asks, so I tell him.

"What hotel are you staying at?" I say that I forget the name of it.

When the song ends he says, "Would you like another dance?" I feel sorry for him, so I shrug, and he continues to dance.

About three drinks and six songs later, the stripper tells me that it's time to get paid. I point in Kellie's direction, and he asks for a huge sum of money, which she refers back to me.

"This is how I make my living," he says. "I asked if you wanted me to keep dancing, and you said yes."

"I'm sorry," I tell him, "I've never been to these places before and didn't know how it worked. I can't pay you all that money. I'm just a high school student."

I tell Kellie that she should chip in, and she's angry because apparently she didn't know how it worked either.

I give the guy a few bills and he says, "I have kids to feed."

I say, "Oh yeah? Then why were you asking for my hotel info?"

It feels so dirty. We duck out the front door as fast as we can and run a mile down the street.

The next afternoon, we get up for breakfast, and I'm

surprisingly not hungover. We head down to a pub on Peel Street and immediately spot a group of good-looking guys. We're seated a few tables away from them and eye each other up throughout our meals. After a couple pitchers of beer, we head over to their table.

Derek is the one that I'm after. He has green eyes, wavy dark hair, and a cunning smirk. It seems that he chose me too.

"I saw you chicks coming in," he says. "I said, 'Nice crappah on the Asian girl.'"

"How romantic," I say. "What a charming pick-up line."

He smiles knowingly.

"That's about the worst thing to call a girl's ass. You know that?" I say.

He shrugs. "What's your name?"

"Millie," I say. "Yeah, yeah—Milli Vanilli—ha ha."

Derek smiles. I feel the nerves in my stomach flit around.

We tell the boys we're going dancing at Club Metropolis later that night, and they promise to meet us. Back at the hotel, I put on pleather shorts and a rhinestone top— something more daring than I'd wear back home. The other girls dress more bravely as well. We're a force when we get to the club. Guys are buying us drink after drink.

My eyes search the multi-tiered club for Derek, but he and his crew are nowhere to be seen. So the girls and I pair off with guys on the floor, sipping and spilling drinks everywhere.

The one I'm dancing with takes me by surprise by flinging me around the room. He's widely mouthing and singing along to the song. *"Why waste your time? You know you're gonna be mine! You know you're gonna be mine! You know you're gonna be mine!"*

He pretends to chase me while singing, "I'm gonna get you baby. I'm gonna get you, yes I am!"

I'm absolutely horrified.

When the song finally ends and my drink is splattered across the floor, he offers to get me another. "Wait right here," he winks and takes off.

As he disappears, Derek arrives looking sharp in a T-shirt and suit jacket.

"Hi," he says. "Do you want to dance?"

I say, "Yes! I've gotta get away from this spot, though, because I was just dancing with the biggest dork!"

He takes my hand and weaves me over the floor to the other side of the club. It feels like an adventure.

We cough through the smoky dry ice with prismed lights pulsing down upon us. I breathe in his soft trail of cologne, look up to his green eyes, and lose myself to the music. It's as if we're the only ones on the floor. Surrounded by smoke, I see no one but him. We dance for an hour straight before grabbing a drink.

As luck would have it, Derek and his friends are also staying at the Holiday Inn. They came with the same tour group on a different bus. He leads me to his room, takes his jacket off my shoulders, and sits down with me on the bed.

When he leans down to kiss me, I feel a mix of nervousness and sparkles in my belly. I haven't felt this way since my last days with Luke. We make out for about forty-five minutes before one of his drunken roommates comes barging in.

"I should go," I tell him. "Can you give me your number?"

"Why don't you give me yours," he says, smiling.

"Okay," I say, thinking nothing of it. I write it down with the pencil on hotel stationary.

"Maybe I'll see you tomorrow," he says.

The girls and I swap stories from the night as we get ready for bed. I tell them how Derek and his friends live just a couple towns over from us. They're excited for the ongoing potential, even though they hooked up with guys elsewhere.

There must be something about Montréal because I wake up the next morning again sans hangover.

Someone turns on the TV. Just as the weatherman displays a big swirling cloud over the entire northeast, there's a knock at our door.

"The bus back is postponed till tomorrow," says the tour group leader. "Big storm happening, and I guess it's even worse back home. Call your parents," he says, and we all cheer with hands in the air.

Happy birthday to me.

"Another night with your sweets!" says Kellie.

I flash her a huge silly smile.

We go back to the same pub again for breakfast, and everything's coming up Millie when we see Derek and his friends being seated there too. We order pitcher upon pitcher of beer and laugh at every stupid thing someone says.

Back at the hotel, I change into black jeans and a white crocheted bra with a matching crocheted top that goes along with it. It doesn't matter that it's a blizzard outside. We're young, foolish, and dressed to impress.

Both groups stumble over to a bar that's playing loud hip-hop. The entire place is raging with kids who are excitedly laid up an extra night. Some of the kids from our school are there, but I ignore them the same way they've always ignored me.

Besides, I've got Derek's full attention. We all jump around with our bottles in the air, trying not to slip on the wet tiles. And when a slow song comes on, he grabs my hand and puts one arm around my waist. I catch a glimpse of myself in the mirrored walls and look pretty damned smitten.

Derek invites me back to his room, and I tell the girls I'll see them all later. Everything before this moment was moving so fast, and now it's like it's all in slow motion. The way he touches my hair and slides his hands around my body feels nothing short of amazing.

"How old are you?" he whispers, as we're kissing.

"I just turned eighteen today." I smile at him.

"Oh yeah? Happy birthday. I've got a present for you," he smirks.

Slowly, very slowly, he undresses me, stopping to put his lips on my skin along the way. We lie sideways on the bed, exploring each other's bodies, gazing deep into eyes, mouths open with wonder.

Maybe this is what I've been waiting for. Maybe this is my reward.

His body is hard all over. He's a hockey player and takes working out seriously. There are ripples down his stomach, lines and crevices that I've never seen in the flesh.

I allow him to take over, and it feels the way I imagine most people would like their first time to be. I pretend, for the moment, it's mine. He holds my hands as we climax almost perfectly in sync.

When I come out of the bathroom in my black jeans and bra, some of his roommates are back. They see Derek topless in his jeans, and for the first time, I do too. I'm so lost staring at him that I don't pay attention to the boys' eyes on me.

"I'll see you later," I say to him, as I grab the last of my clothes.

"I'll call you," he says, chest thumping.

THE OMEN

Back in Massachusetts, Kellie, Derek, and his friend, who Kellie likes, are sitting on my bedroom floor. We're listening to music and talking a little about Montréal and the hockey team that the boys play on.

Derek wants to know what I do and I shrug.

"Millie writes songs and stories," says Kellie.

"Oh yeah?" Derek says, interest piqued.

"Well, I used to," I say, jabbing Kellie with my foot.

"Why'd you stop?" he asks.

"I don't know. Lack of inspiration," I say, because it's not exactly a lie.

"When did you stop, Cutie?" Kellie says. Cutie is one of her nicknames for me when she's not calling me bitch or slut.

"I work on stuff here and there but not regularly anymore." I lie this time.

"I'd love to see and hear it," Derek says.

"What else do you do?" I say, deflecting, looking up into his eyes.

"I write poetry sometimes," he says easily.

"Fag," jokes his friend. I frown at him.

"Will you write something for me?" I ask.

"Maybe someday," he says. "You got any paper?"

I hand him a piece of red construction paper and a black pen. He doodles while we continue to talk. When they leave, I go back to my room and look at the red paper.

Eyes so dark, hair so wild. How I've missed your pretty smile, it says, along with a little sketch of me. I hold the paper to my chest and smile.

Derek wants to meet at a secret location. I get out of my car and into his. I dressed pretty for him and wore a nice shade of red on my lips. It reminds me of the red paper.

"You look amazing," he says, gazing at me.

I smile shyly and say, "Thanks. You look cute." But his smile disappears.

He says, "Look, there's something I need to tell you."

My heart drops. He doesn't like me. This is it.

"What?" I say, full of hesitation.

He takes a few moments, looks out the window at nothing, and says, "I've got a chick."

Splat. From fifteen stories up, my heart drops like glass.

"You... you do?" I manage. "Since when?" I ask, wondering who upstaged me.

We've been together two years," he says.

"Two years?" I repeat, feeling salt in the wound. "So in Montréal?"

He nods his head slowly. "We hadn't been getting along. I thought it was gonna end. Things aren't like they used to be with me and her. I dunno. It's confusing."

"What's confusing?" I ask.

"I don't know what to do," he says sadly. "There I was in Montréal and met this beautiful girl who happens to live so close by... But I've known her for two years. I chased her for a whole year before she'd even look at me. She didn't want to be with me because she's a smart girl, and I'm a hockey player. She hates hockey players," he says.

"Why are you telling me all this?" I say, wishing he wouldn't share so much. "I already feel bad enough."

"It's not your fault, it's mine," he says. "I should've told you sooner."

"So do you want to stop seeing me?" I say, feeling crushed.

"I dunno," he says. He looks at me and says, "No. But I should."

"So what does that mean?" I say, confused.

"I just feel like I could have something with you, but I don't know you well enough. It's bad timing," he says.

"There I was thinking it was perfect timing," I sulk.

"Maybe we should get together now and then. I dunno. Get to know each other better," he says.

"So you can decide who's better?" I ask, feeling insulted and oddly up to the challenge.

He shrugs. "I dunno. It's not fair, is it?"

"No," I say to him. "Not for anyone but you."

He puts his head down, and I can see how hard this is for him. I think to myself, *Well, he didn't have to tell me.*

"But I'll do it," I say. "I'll still see you if that's all it is. No sex."

The next time I meet Derek in his car, it's raining out.

We look up through the sunroof and the windshield as the rain drops down above us. The music's loud enough to feel, and we both sit with each other in silence, taking all the beauty in. We don't talk. We just hover right here in this limbo we've both agreed to be in together.

A few songs in, we catch each other's eye at the right moment. He lowers the music.

"What are you thinking about," he asks.

"Just life," I say. "How much we think we know in a moment and then realize we don't a moment later."

"Sounds depressing," he says, "but I know what you mean."

"I guess I'm a depressing girl," I say. "If you only knew."

"What is it?" he asks.

"Nothing," I say honestly. "It's complicated enough already."

"I guess," he says.

The third time we meet, he makes the mistake of kissing me. I make the mistake of giving him oral sex. The both of us should've known better, but we were so overwhelmed by all that we weren't saying.

"Shit," he says, cooling off, wiping lipstick off himself. "If my chick finds out, she'll be pissed."

And in that moment, I decide that I'm angry with him. I don't like the way he calls her his "chick" and refers to her in front of me—especially after what we've just done. It feels rude to the both of us. And I don't like that his first instinct is to cover it up rather than tell her he found someone new.

But for some reason, I continue to see Derek. I can't really understand or justify it. It's not the same though. In my heart—or what's left of it—I have written him off from being my great romance. I still find him attractive but have lost the rosy filter I used to look at him with. He's lost my respect, and it hurts to acknowledge.

I hear from Kellie that Derek's team has a game, so a bunch of us decide to go. It's outside on a chilled rink. We drive up and blast the same stations from car radios as if it's the stadium sound.

A truck full of guys pulls up blaring the same station. Some are sitting in back of the pickup, singing along to the music. When this rap duet comes on, I jump in for the girl parts while this cute redhead jumps in for the guy parts. I've never seen a redheaded guy I found attractive before, but there's just something about this one. And we've got mad chemistry, as everyone can see.

Both crowds cheer us on as we go instead of watching the game. He's the Kid to my Play. We switch off almost too perfectly, enjoying the energy we build between us. When it's over, he tells me his name is Damien.

"Like the devil?" I smirk.

"You got it," he smirks back.

We drink cans of beer in the lot with our friends, paying half-attention to the game and the other half to each other. I give Damien my number when he asks for it and feel good about meeting someone new. Derek's obviously in no rush to choose me over his *chick*, and I'm not sure I'd trust him if he left her now anyway.

CUT FROM
THE SAME CLOTH

The guidance counselor at school wants to meet. It's mandatory to talk to seniors about their plans after graduation. We met a couple years back, after *The Incident,* when I was sent to the principal's office. She's the one who had a fight on the phone with my mother. It feels weird going back into her office again.

"Have you given much thought toward your future, Mille?" she asks sweetly.

I shake my head. "No, I can't say that I have," I say honestly.

"I can see your grades have suffered a lot," she says, looking over my file with a furrowed brow. "The first semester of freshman year you were nearly straight As. Now you're all C's with a couple of D's and one F."

I nod my head without offering apologies or excuses.

"Is this the best you think you can do?" she asks.

I nod my head again, wondering if she remembers me at all. It's not like there are so many other Asians in this school.

"What do you think you'd like to do when you graduate?" she asks.

"Move away," I say. "I don't really care where."

"You could go away to college," she says, "after maybe completing a year at a community college to get your grades back up."

"I'm not gonna do that," I tell her. "Besides, my family has no money."

"I'm sure that they could help you out with some school," she says sternly, peering over her glasses. "And you could get a part-time job to round it out."

I sit in silence.

"What do you like, Millie? Do you still like music?" she says. "Didn't you sing a song you wrote at one of the Carnival Balls?"

"I don't want to do music anymore," I tell her. "I like art."

"Well, unfortunately there's not much you can do with that," she says, disappointed. "There's commercial art, but you've gotta be really good to make it."

I give her nothing.

"Look, if you're not gonna go to school, that's fine, but you need to start thinking about your future," she says. "Most of the kids have already chosen their top schools and received acceptance letters. You should be thinking more seriously about this stuff."

I nod and get up to leave.

There was a time when I begged for this day to come: a discussion about getting the fuck out and on with my life. But honestly, I can't think of one single thing I'd like to do for the rest of my life. It's hard to imagine a "rest of my life" as I struggle with my day-to-day.

I tell my mother that they're asking me about college and she says, "And what'd you tell them?"

"I'm not going," I say.

"Huh," she says and leaves it at that.

I guess my parents recently found a bank account that my father doesn't remember opening. It has both his and my aunt's name on it, meaning she may have used it to cash checks made out to him. They have some sort of investigator on the job now, and it's not looking good for anyone. Lots of money has gone through, but not a lot of money is left to be found.

The last concern on my parents' minds is where I'm going to college with money no one has.

Damien calls one day after school, and his voice is so raspy and cute. He wants to meet up and get the crews both together. I call the girls, and we make plans to meet at someone's house.

We spend the night drinking and laughing with some game on in the background. There are a few synchronized cheers and grunts, but it's otherwise a pretty good time. I'm not into sports and neither are my girls, so we roll our eyes whenever the boys stop midsentence to react.

Damien and I end up making out in a room together. He's got a feistiness about him. He's all raw expression, and it's nice to feel wanted again.

It's been a while, so I'm just as anxious as he is to feel

the justification that having sex with someone cute brings. It's not the best sex I've ever had, but I enjoy it because it's with him. Perhaps I like the idea of having sex with him more than the feeling, but it's more than good enough for the time being.

When we're laying in a sweaty mess, he asks how I met his crew.

I tell him, "The girls and I met some of your friends in Montréal in March. Then we heard about the game we all met you at. That's pretty much it."

"Oh yeah?" he says. "I was supposed to go on that trip, but I had to stay back last minute. Too bad because I could've met you up there," he says, smirking.

"Well, you met me now," I say, smirking back.

"Did you meet my brother up there?" he asks.

"I dunno, who's your brother?" I ask.

"Derek," he says.

I freeze up, completely dumbfounded.

"What's the matter?" he asks.

"Derek's your brother?" I say. "But you don't look anything alike."

"Why? Is that a problem?" he asks, confused.

I don't know if he knows about his brother cheating on his girlfriend with me, so I hesitate to say anything. But then I remember that he was also cheating on me with his girlfriend before I even knew about her.

After pausing for just a little too long, I say, "I slept with your brother."

"You're shittin' me," Damien says with the straightest face I've ever seen on him.

I shake my head, "No, but I wish I was."

SHAME ON ME

The girls all find my situation hilarious. They say it serves Derek right for lying about his girlfriend and that Damien and I make a better couple. I explain to them that Damien and I can't be a couple now, given the news. But the girls don't see the problem.

Never mind the situation. Even if Damien wasn't Derek's brother, it's not the same as it was with Derek. Derek and I had a true beginning. It was romantic—if he didn't have a girlfriend back home.

Shit.

Damien and I get along too well to be that kind of couple. He's a good-time guy, and I'm a good-time girl. We have fun like a couple of buds that just happen to like having sex.

I know I shouldn't feel bad about Derek. After leading me on and lying to his *chick*, he can't possibly be mad. Besides, there's no way I could have ever guessed that Damien was his brother. Derek's got a slim frame, brown hair, and green eyes. Damien's stockier with red hair, hazel eyes, and freckles. One's loud and the other is quiet. They're as different as two people could be and still be brothers. Well, aside from the example of me and *my* family.

Maybe one is adopted?

Damien's given me his number—their number—and when someone picks up, I realize I can't tell if it's Damien or Derek. I never noticed how similar their voices are until now. Always having the accompanying visual, it never occurred to me.

"Who's this?" I ask.

"Does it matter?" the voice says.

"Yes, it does," I say.

"Who do you want it to be?" the voice asks.

"It must be Derek," I say, thinking Damien would never make such a big deal.

The phone clicks, and there's just dial tone. So apparently Derek cares.

I feel like I've managed to hit a new low, despite it not being one-hundred-percent my fault. Intel was kept from me. Had I known all the facts, perhaps it wouldn't have happened.

If you'd kept your legs closed, there'd be no problem.

Shut up, little voice. You're supposed to be on my side.

Derek stops calling to meet up at our secret location. We ignore each other when our paths cross at parties and events. I even get to see his *chick* at a party. His nerves jump when he sees me walk in. He doesn't know I have too much tact to say something. Besides, it's his job to break her heart, not mine.

Damien and I continue to hang out. It's just easy and

uncomplicated. Neither of us appears to want more than we've got, and it's refreshing. I have a hard time getting pleasured by him though. There's just something missing. We've tried different scenarios, but it's never quite there.

One weekend, we all go up to Montréal again. It's a little weird after meeting his brother there, but they're such different people, and it's a much different time. We do it hanging out the fifth-story window one night, and I hold on for dear life, afraid I might plummet to my death buck naked. It's kind of hot with the risk factor and all, but still, I don't come. I never tell him but he knows. He talks about having his friend join us sometime, but I'm not sure I want to elevate to that level of slutdom.

The girls and I go out to a bar in Boston now that they've got fake IDs too. We have a few beers and talk to a few guys, but no one appeals to us. I decide to get one more beer, and a bouncer asks for my ID. He takes it away and kicks me out, unable to let the others know.

I wait around outside for what seems like hours. It's getting chilly, and I'm only wearing a short-sleeved dress. A couple of guys come up and start chatting with me. They say they only live a couple towns over and offer me a ride home.

The room is dark and the air feels so thick that I can't breathe. Then I realize there's someone on top of me. I feel the sharp pain of penetration. I freak out.

"No! Stop! What are you doing? Stop!" I shout, and he backs off.

Someone else comes into the room and says, "What are you doing to her?"

"Nothing!" he yells defensively. "I thought she wanted

to. She was going along with it until she started screaming!"

"I was sleeping!" I say, crying now. "Bring me home! Please!"

"Okay! All right!" the guy says.

In the car, I give brief directions from the backseat as the two of them sit in front in silence. I carefully wipe the stubborn tears from my eyes so they don't smear my makeup. I get out of the car without a thanks, but I don't slam the door, nor do I look back.

With Maggie in my bed purring on me, I pat his soft, silky fur and cry silently to myself. I pride myself on never crying. I don't understand my own tears or emotions. I have no idea what happened or why we detoured to that house. All I know was they were taking me home, and I woke up with a stranger inside me.

There's a saying that my father always uses, and it pisses me off as I hear his words in my head: "Fool me once, shame on you. Fool me twice, shame on me."

I decide to tell no one about this.

EDGING

I used to do this thing when I was little. I'd get up in the middle of the night and listen to the silence—the sweet, rare silence—in the house. I'd hear the clock in the front room, ticking faithfully; my father snoring; and the random little noises that pass unnoticed in the loud house any other time.

I stand in the kitchen, directly in front of the TV. The little monitors are just to my right. You can't really make out a picture in most of them unless a TV or a light is left on in a room. I stand here because, now at hip height, is the cutlery drawer.

Sometimes I study the knives for too long. I inspect the rust on a steak knife here and there. I gently push one into a fingertip to test for its sharpness. I wonder who used that knife last.

Once I select the right knife, I close the drawer and just stand there with it in my hand. There have been times when I've held it against my belly, right between my rib cage. Other times I've just squeezed on the handle, balancing the tip of it on the pale pink countertop.

The ticks of my parents' wedding clock lull me into a daze that intensifies over time. I feel the heat generating from clenched muscles reach my head. I hear the pressure of a voice—a voice of mine in my head that doesn't sound like me—taunt, *Do it, you coward! Why can't you just do it? You're so weak, you stupid chink!*

When all the heat and the pressure push in on my head, I squeeze my abs to keep from convulsing. I fight back the tears with everything I've got left.

I split in two. One half is a bully, and the other half is too stubborn to be overtaken.

One half prays for the courage to bear down on the knife and stick it so deeply into my body. It visualizes my collapse as the blood pours out all around me while I fade out and away from the pain.

The other half visualizes the faces of my mother, the quiet brother, and my baby brother. Somehow I don't think I can do it to them. It's not fair to have three against one. I know you're not supposed to care because when you're dead, you can't. Yet guilt and the feeling of dying misunderstood always get to me.

My mother—I think she's despised me since that time she found my diary when I was a kid. When I look in her face, I believe there's a part of her who wants to love me and perhaps feels guilty that she can't. Maybe I'm just too foreign to her.

At some point, the energy all transfers from my body back to my head. The intensity steadies to a numb. I put the knife in the drawer and retreat like a zombie back to my room. I forget about it till the next time.

PLAYING GROWN-UP

A week after graduation, my mother swings by my room and asks, "So what are your plans? You can't just do nothing for the rest of your life. Are you going to get a job or what?"

My whole life is supposedly in front of me now. I have nothing but options and choices. Funny how it doesn't feel that way.

"I'll figure something out," I say to her. But I don't think she believes me.

I surprise her two weeks later when I say I met a guy at a party who told me he does this thing called temping. You take a few tests at an office, and they hook you up with short-term office jobs. I figure it'll let me see what kinds of work there is out there since I haven't a clue where to start otherwise. She's very impressed by this.

My oldest sister has been making huge improvements, meaning her weight and moods are stabilizing. She's struggling with not being able to fit into a size zero anymore, but I'm thankful she still has clothes in her old size six.

In my sister's suit, I show up at the temp office and whiz through the tests with flying colors. I grew up on computers, so there's nothing I can't easily learn, and my typing is lightning fast. The only thing that I find myself deficient in is that high-pitched, cheery demeanor they beg of me.

"Let's do a little role playing," says the white-haired Jewish woman. "I'll go first. Just say hello as I walk through the door."

She walks out and back in, and I manage a stifled, "Hello."

She says, "Hi! I'm Millie! How are you?" all upswing. "Can you do that?" she asks, shaking my hand with vigor. "Go ahead. Go out that door, and you be you now."

I walk in the door and she says, "Hello," and I say, "Hi. I'm Millie. How are you?" with a half-smile.

She says, "No, no, no, no," and shakes her head. "You need to have a smile *in* your voice. Like this, 'Hi! I'm Millie! How are you?' Can you hear the difference?"

I nod my head as she swats me back out the door. I feel like a loser, but I force myself through it. I walk in and meet her somewhere halfway. It's like a bad acting class, but it pleases her, thank Christ.

And so the process begins of going on interviews and returning hours later like a douche with personalized thank you notes. Before I know it, I'm wearing suits every day, taking the T, and working in law firms, private health care offices, and something called reinsurance.

Suddenly I'm being treated well by everyone I meet. As it turns out, people really do judge a book by its cover. And,

as it turns out, I enjoy the way it feels to be given the benefit of the doubt.

My parents couldn't be prouder, and it's been many
years since I last felt their warm smiles beaming down onto
me. I'd forgotten what it was like. In fact, I nearly forget
what it was like just weeks prior—before I became this picture of success.

"You're so young, and you've really got it together," say
the people two and three times my age at my temp jobs.

I smile politely but think to myself, *You have no idea.*

When I learn that one company wants to hire me full-
time, I might as well have received the Nobel Peace Prize at
home. It's like a Cinderella story, an overnight success.
They can't believe how quickly I've completely changed my
life.

Since the taste of success first tickles me, a new confidence arises. I turn down that full-time job when I learn of
another opening that the recruiter says is way out of my
league. Coincidentally, it's not through her.

"Have you forgotten where you came from?" the white
haired woman asks. "I put in all that work with you," she
says bitterly.

If I don't take the job being offered through her, she
doesn't receive the big fat check. She tries to knock me
down as I'm learning to walk on my own. I keep my cool
and let her unravel over the phone but tell her that I appreciate her help, now goodbye.

I get the other job for over five thousand dollars more.
It's a big insurance company, so there are other employees
closer to my age. Nobody's as young as eighteen, but there
are some late-twenty-somethings. They treat me as equals

and are fortunate for a little more youth in a company full of middle-aged suits.

There's this one woman, Deanna, who's not keen on my youth. She's a lead administrator, and from what I gather, she's not keen on much. She's unabashedly competitive, complains all day long and puts down everyone with subtle jabs. I decide that she's my new example of everything I don't ever want to become.

The work is a little challenging, but I can't imagine being here for more than a couple of years before turning into a Deanna. There's only so much I can learn about making spreadsheets, coding claims, arranging travel, and picking up other people's lunch. It's the respect and the paycheck that I enjoy at my age, really. It's the sudden effect of looking like I'm not a throwaway. No one in this new world knows me from my old world. No one knows that I'm broken.

REDUX

High on my new life, I finally make the bold move to call Luke.

"Hello" is all he says to send nerves shooting through me like a drug.

"Hi. Remember me?" I say confidently.

"Millie! Of course. I was wondering what happened to you," he says.

"Then why didn't you call to find out?" I say teasingly.

"I don't know," he says honestly. "Did you have a good summer—um, year?"

"It's been crazy," I tell him. "Last summer was a blast. Best ever. The rest of the year was kind of meh, but I got through it. Been to Montréal a couple of times. Just got a new job."

"Oh yeah? Good for you. What are you doing?" he says.

"I'm the Senior Secretary of the products department of an insurance company in Boston," I say with a smile, feeling full of myself.

"No shit? Big shot now, eh?" he says.

"I have to wear a suit every day. It's kind of lame, but you'd be amazed at how well people treat a girl in a suit."

"I bet," he says.

"What are you up to these days? Do you want to get together? Or..." I say, voice trailing. This is when he's supposed to tell me if he has a girlfriend. *A chick.*

"Sure, yeah," he says. My heart swoons. "What's a good night?"

"I get home around six," I say. "My week is open."

"How about I pick you up on Thursday," he says. "Same house?"

"Sadly, yes," I tell him.

"See you around six thirty," he says.

I almost want to wear a suit to impress him but realize how uncool that is. So I put on a black and white striped bodysuit with a red skirt and black boots. I dab on some red lip gloss to pull it all together.

Eagerly, I sit on my front doorstep trying to look relaxed as I twirl a dying flower between my fingers. And as the old-man sedan slows down and pulls into the top of the driveway, I rise to take my first walk in over a year to greet him. Legs swinging slowly with intention, he steps out of the car with a smile.

When he comes around the side to hold the door open for me, our eyes lock for a beat or two. I slide my legs in with a smirk.

"You look great. The year has agreed with you," he says nicely.

"Your skin is nice and brown from the summer," I say

to him. "Your eyes look so blue."

He smiles, "Thanks. Where should we go? Are you hungry?"

"Not really," I say, looking down at his lips. "Maybe somewhere private?"

"Okay," he says. "I know where we can go."

We pull into a clearing in the woods a couple towns over. He stops the car. "Is this okay?"

"Perfect," I say, turning in my seat to gaze at him. "So how has your year been?"

"It's been okay," he says. "I'm working now as an electrician. It should be good once I get into the union."

"That's great," I say, eyes tracing his features.

He leans over and touches my hair, turning my face toward his. When we kiss, I feel a surge of nervous energy flitter throughout my body.

"Hey, you wouldn't have any weed, would you?" I ask.

"You're smoking now?" he says. "Yeah, I have a little one hitter. Not sure how much is in it."

Luke opens a compartment in the car and fishes out the wooden device and starts examining it. "Ladies first," he says, handing it to me with a lighter.

I take two hits, and Luke takes one before it's spent. "Good enough for me," I say, smiling.

He puts it away and we start kissing again.

There's so much I want to share with him—too much. I want him to know how much I've improved. There's an urgent desire to feed him everything all at once, and I can hardly contain myself.

We crawl into the back, and I climb on top of him. It's kind of frantic—nothing like the calculated ways he orchestrated all of those past times. I take control, unzipping his pants and slipping out of my underwear. He grabs a condom and in no time at all, we're going at it like crazy.

"You're fucking wild," he says, smiling.

"Yeah," I whisper, not wanting to stop.

It's so much yet not enough and all so very soon. I start coming and coming consecutively until he finishes, and we end up panting on each other's off-beat. I hold on to him with my chin over his shoulder for a while. And then I realize we should probably dress in case anyone else comes around.

I find myself in the front seat zoning out. Luke is talking, but I can't seem to keep anything straight. By the time he finishes a sentence, I've already forgotten the beginning.

Maybe a half-hour later when I'm sobering up Luke says to me, "Can I tell you something?"

"What?" I say wearily.

"I don't think you should smoke weed," he says.

"Why would you say that? You do," I offer.

"It doesn't seem to do good things for you," he says. "You've kind of been off in another world since we finished. It's been like an hour."

"I have? I'm sorry," I say. "I didn't realize. Maybe it's just this stuff. I'm not used to it."

"Maybe," he says skeptically.

"Can you get some for me if I need it?" I ask. "I'm all out of what my friends in Maine sent me home with."

"Yeah, if you really want it," he says. "But think about it."

By the time he drops me back home, I'm dead weight.

"Thanks, Luke," I say, clumsily climbing out of the car.

MALFUNCTION

I'm mildly depressed the next day at work. It was wonderful to see Luke again. And I had so much to prove, but I totally blew it. I feel like such an ass for bragging about how well I'm doing one moment and then falling apart in the next.

He's right. That weed really didn't do me justice. Things were going so well before I asked if he had any. Why did I need to get fucked up in order to be with him? It could've gone so much better if I hadn't.

Idiot!

It's kind of a relief when we're told that we're spending the last four hours of the day at a mandatory company meeting. I can't really focus on doing work anyhow. We file down to this huge room full of chairs and suits while a balding man stands stiffly by a projector screen. He thanks us for being there and wants to start with a video, he says. So the lights go down and the screen lights up.

Another balding white man in a suit is projected onto

the screen. Audio of a man's voice starts to play. My eyes wander around the room, wondering what's going on. Clearly someone forgot to hit play. However, no one else seems to be affected, as this unmoving picture of a man smiles at us while he "talks." It's like watching a disobedient ventriloquist dummy.

Oh no. Don't laugh. Please. Don't.

My eyes—still scanning the room in disbelief—land upon one man fighting to stifle his own laughter. And then I lose it. I start bouncing silently in my chair with the back of my hand pressed into my mouth, convulsing with laughter that threatens to burst through any second. I can't even look around me to see if anyone's noticing—because surely they do. I'm afraid that if I catch someone's eye, I'll fall to the floor wailing.

The "video" seems to go on forever. Every time I think I'm in the clear, I look up and lose it again and again. I've even forgotten what I find so hysterical about it. I'm not sure if it's the actual "video," the fact that it's been passed off as one, or the fact that everyone else seems perfectly okay with believing it is one.

When the lights finally come on and the man standing begins to speak, I think I've got it back under control. He tells us all why that man is such a glowing inspiration. He's our founder, the one who made all of our jobs possible. He took the company public and made so many rich. The room applauds.

Call it cruel humanity, but I totally lose it again. I start coughing to cover it up. My eyes are tearing so badly that I bury my face in my hands, bending forward into my lap. I manage to dig out a tissue with one hand and cover my face, hoping to just disappear.

When I finally recover on the train back home, I wonder if the rest of the company is so numbed by corporate bull-shit to be affected anymore. It's funny how some people can adjust to insanity to the point of not realizing they're in it.

JAMES

Unsurprisingly, Luke hasn't been calling. He must've found me a depressing sight. I've been hanging with the girls and sleeping with Damien here and there. But there's this feeling—like a growing void—somewhere between my stomach and chest.

I remember feeling this way as a kid. It's an awkward feeling of limbo—like I don't really fit with my past but don't really belong in my present. Every breath that swirls down into my lungs exhales an anxiousness that I can't quite place. The future feels promising in some abstract sense. I can't see it but can't wait to be in it. Present day is like watching someone else go through the motions—those expected of me. It's an odd mix of security and stifled discontent. Perhaps I feel more like who I was before *The Incident* happened.

There's this guy who manages the car wash I go to after work every other week. My dad says that since I bought a car, I must take care of it. Fair enough. Anyway, this brown-haired blue-eyed guy, about a foot taller than me, pays me special attention. He gives me free add-ons and smiles. I don't find him particularly attractive, but there's something about him. Maybe it's the gentlemanly gestures mixed with the masked nervousness.

One night, as the boys towel-dry my car, he leans into my window. He says, "Hi. I think you're super beautiful and would love to take you to dinner sometime." It's completely rushed and rehearsed-sounding.

Caught off guard, my gut reaction is to just say, "Sure. Okay."

"Can I have your number so I can call you?" he asks. And of course, he pulls out a pen and paper, ever-prepared like a Boy Scout.

When James picks me up at the door in a silk patterned shirt, I manage a smile while cringing behind my own face. His hair is brushed perfectly into a slight wave, and he smells of a little too much cologne. Instead of jeans he wears *slacks*. And he's holding one dozen long-stemmed red roses.

He's got the shiniest car ever, of course. The interior is so Armor All-ed that I wish I'd brought sunglasses. But ever the gentleman he is, opening and shutting my door for me. It feels almost too normal until he finds himself in a nervous cycle.

"This girl I was dating before, she was really nice but controlling. I was like, 'Uh, I don't see no rings on these fingers,'" he says, lifting his left hand off the wheel for effect. "Uh, I don't see no rings on these fingers," he repeats. The first time I thought it was peculiar, but the third and fourth time he repeats it, I want to roll down the window and jump.

I try calming him down.

"So where did you grow up?" I ask, allowing him to take a few breaths.

He doesn't live too far from Luke, but he's about six years older than me. I hadn't realized, but it half-explains his style.

"Can I ask you a question?" he says.

"Sure," I say hesitantly.

"Why is your last name Vaniti? Is your mom Asian and your dad Italian or what?"

"I was adopted from Korea," I tell him. "I was six months old."

I'm prepared for the onslaught of follow-up questions but instead he says, "Huh. I was adopted too."

"You were?" I say, shocked. I've only ever met one other white adoptee, and he was the brother of the only other Korean adoptee I've met.

"Yeah," he says. "I was three months old. And I have a younger sister from South America."

"Wow," I say.

"She was three years old. She used to hide food under her bed. As soon as my parents adopted her, they babied her and forgot about me," he says. "She had a tougher beginning," he adds, to excuse his parents. I know how that works.

"Do you know about *your* beginning?" I ask.

"Yeah," he says. "My birth mother was a teenager from Boston. I guess if I ever want to know, I can find out who she is. I don't wanna, though. I'm all set."

Just like that, this goofy and questionably dressed guy and I have something in common. I'd never been on a date with another adoptee before.

We talk more about our families and adoptions over dinner in a small Italian restaurant. Although our stories are completely different, it's nice to talk with someone who has some understanding of an undisclosed part of me. There's a comfort, an honesty, that I've never felt with anyone.

Over the next few weeks, James takes on the challenge of being The Most Romantic Man I've Ever Dated. Little does he know that by bringing me flowers on our first date, he's already won. Nonetheless, he plans laborious scavenger hunts, continually finds my car in huge garages to surprise me with a rose on my windshield, and writes me love letters every day.

There's an intensity radiating off him that burns my skin a little. It's an unavoidable force that disallows me to gather my feelings of him as a person. Having somebody dote on me to this extent feels cruel to abandon. And topping it off with his being an adoptee and the sex—well, he wins.

"You don't have to make yourself like him, you know," says Kellie to me about James.

"I'm not," I say, but I'm not sure it's the truth. "There are a lot of weird things but, I don't know, we have something special. We were both adopted."

Given that we're both living at home until he goes back to school next month, finding decent places to have sex is difficult. James knows of a fancy underground hotel that caters to people like us.

Our bed is heart-shaped with red satin sheets. The lights

are red, and there's a hot tub bubbling in the corner. James opens the bottle of sparkling wine and pours me a glass. He sits atop the red sheets in another patterned silk shirt that has too many buttons undone. I instantly feel like I've entered the set of a porno from the seventies.

"What's wrong, Millie?" he asks, with a face of concern.

"Nothing," I say, biting my lip. How do I tell him that everything about this place is cheesy, and that I hate his shirt and the way he's wearing it?

"You just look unhappy," he says.

If I could, I would snap out of this weird feeling and appreciate him for what he is. He's the sweetest, most passionate guy I've ever met. But he loves me so hard that I can't even breathe, nor see him for who he is under that shirt.

We get high and laugh a lot together. We go hiking through the White Mountains and have sex up against trees. We play cards and listen to music. So long as I'm drunk or high or having sex, things are good.

The truth is, reservations about James aside, there's a freedom that I have with him like no other. He's attentive and does all the fairytale things men are supposed to do for the woman they love, according to Disney and Hollywood. I convince myself that I'm just not used to being with a good guy and let him carry me away with his persistence.

Once I start staying weekends at James's school, he starts talking to me while I sleep.

"Millie, will you marry me?" he whispers.

I stay silent and keep pretending to sleep. He repeats the question, and I wonder about it.

Is this what I'm supposed to do now—marry him? Is that

what good girls are supposed to do? Is this my chance to be painted white again?

Every night that I stay over, when he's not too drunk to do so, he plays this game with my subconscious.

"Millie, will you marry me?" he says lowly.

Then one night—maybe it's the weed or the booze—or maybe I just want to be in love, but I let out a quiet, "Yes."

PULLING THE TRIGGER

My parents are smitten with James. When he stays over, he talks with my mom for hours after I've gone to bed. He's been singing my praises to her, knowing it'll all come back to me. He's building a following so that it's impossible for me to say no to him.

I have to admit, if I'm being completely honest, that making my parents happy feels like incentive enough to be with him. On some level, I realize how lame that is, yet I can't quell my need for their approval.

James thinks that he's sly, talking to me hypothetically about wedding proposals. I'm still not sure about him but can't stomach the idea of upsetting him. There's so much good inside him—I can see that. There's an innocence—a boy who just needs to be loved. What kind of girl would hurt someone like that?

When we're high, I tell him I want the fairytale of being surprised by a horse and carriage. I imagine us riding through the park during sunset. He'll stop the driver and get down on one knee. I lead him on but no more than myself. Truth is, I haven't thought about marriage since *The Incident* happened, so I just tell him what I thought I wanted when I was a little girl.

One day I decide I better tell him about *The Incident*. It's awkward and awful, really, the way he looks at me as I tell him.

"Did you scream? Did you fight him? Did you say no?" he asks, all in quick succession.

"Well, I," I say, searching for the right words. "I don't think I did scream or say no but I fought back. It was scary and happened so fast. He had a gun. I was afraid to make things worse."

"What could possibly be worse?" he says, followed by, "I'm sorry. I just can't believe you didn't say no."

Later on that night, on our way to a party, we stop off at a liquor store. Underage, I wait in the car. James gets out, shuts the door, and then turns around to face me through the open window.

He says, "Do you wanna see my gun?"

I look at him with shock and awe. His face contorts and he says, "Oh my God! I don't know why I just said that!" He turns around and heads into the store.

Since our first date, I've known that James has some strange communicative issues. He's quite emotionally unaware. I forgive him for his strange and crude outburst because I figure he's trying to deal with *The Incident* being part of my history. However, I can't say it goes unnoticed that once again, I'm the one making excuses for why it's hard for others to deal with what happened to me.

On our first anniversary at the beginning of August, James says he'll pick me up from work to take me to dinner. It's a scorching hot day, and my heels are literally sinking into the sidewalk as I wait patiently. There's a lot of traffic in the city, and he's running really late—so late that I duck back into the office to cool off every few minutes.

Eventually James shows up with two dozen red roses that barely fit in the car. He's broken out into a sweat. I can see that he's tense, so I don't say much.

"I'm sorry I made you wait so long," he says. "There was just too much traffic. I wasn't prepared."

"It's all right," I say. "I'm in the AC now. Where are we going?"

"It's a surprise," he says, managing a half-smile.

There's an increased unsteadiness about him as we seem to meander for an hour around back roads. Every now and then he bangs his palm against the steering wheel. His face reddens when I look at him, so I try to stare out the window at nothing in particular. Eventually we pull into my driveway.

I'm confused. "Aren't we going to dinner?" I say.

"Change of plans. We'll go to dinner a little later," he says.

We get out of the car, and he walks behind me. I catch him doing a funny dance with his arms.

"What are you *doing?*" I ask, weirded out.

"I'm just brushing something off my shirt," he says.

My bedroom is downstairs now, through the garage door. We go in, and I start powdering my sweaty face. James is acting shifty.

"What's going *on,* James?" I ask again, sitting on the

edge of my bed.

James comes over and starts kissing me. He leans me back so my head's on the pillow and says, "Happy anniversary."

"Happy anniversary," I echo, still confused.

Then he pulls a little box out of his pocket and opens it for me. "This isn't how it was supposed to go," he says, "but will you marry me?"

All of a sudden, everything starts to click. My mind's going so fast I can't think.

"Are you gonna say yes?" he says, holding the ring out.

He slides the ring onto my finger. I look up to his child-like eyes of wonder, afraid to crush the moment he's hoping will suffice.

I hear myself say, "Yes," and let him kiss and make love to me. The entire time, I'm wondering in my head about what I've done.

As we're dressing, he tells me how he'd planned on arriving in a horse and buggy, but the Humane Society had shut down all the drivers due to extreme heat. Then, on the way home, he was panicking, trying to find another place to propose, but there were children running through all the parks. My family was expecting to barrage us with Champagne and chocolates when we pulled into the driveway—which was why he signaled in the surveillance cameras to call it off.

"They probably think you said no," he says frantically. "Quick—let's go tell them you said yes!"

He grabs my hand, and we hurry up the stairs to a bunch of confused faces. We all listen to James retell the comedy of errors. We drink Champagne and laugh together and, for a second, I almost believe that what I'm doing is right.

TWENTY
GOING ON FORTY

James's mother's father is said to be a self-made millionaire. He's got property all over Boston. To save on taxes, his
accountant advised him to give each of his relatives ten
thousand dollars. So, without ever renting an apartment
together, we're told it's a smarter investment to buy a
condo instead since we're engaged to be married. With my
job and his down payment, it's surprisingly easy to do.

We end up in a luxurious-looking place on a river, complete with a fitness center and indoor swimming pool. We
don't realize at the time of closing that we're the youngest
residents, as the majority of the occupants are retirees.

Since we had nothing to start off with, we'd arranged
with the sellers to buy some of their furnishings. I find myself looking around at this mauve place with mirrored cabinets, glass tables, and black lacquer furniture. I begin to feel

like a middle-aged Italian housewife.

It seems like overnight I've become a twenty-year-old engaged condo owner with a boring nine-to-five desk job. I have an overbearing, judgmental mother-in-law and a condo association dictating what color curtains I can have. Thank God for the cat.

We adopt Jasminn just as soon as we can, without so much as a photograph, because we heard she was going to be euthanized. She's an older cat whose owner had died, and no one else would claim her. My heart went out to her on the verge of death by unfair circumstances. We fax papers and pass phone interviews during work hours and have her home within moments of the needle. They nearly euthanized her anyway because we were a half-hour past their deadline, the bastards.

The first night she's home, I wake up to a heavy weight on my stomach. When I open my eyes, it's her, belly-to-belly with me, purring in my face. At this moment I become her mother. From somewhere deeper than our uncertain pasts, we connect through the beauty of the present. I know I'll do anything to love and protect her.

It's this complete adoration for Jasminn and all her clumsy discoveries that keep me afloat. Someone at the shelter thought it was wise to declaw her at eight years old to better her chances of finding a new home. Her footing is off as she explores the apartment, which brings much-needed comic relief to my otherwise dreadful transition into adulthood.

James's mother is throwing books of wedding etiquette at us, and his father keeps spouting golden rules and rules of thumb. It's never-ending—the advice and the criticism we receive.

My parents are surprisingly easy through it all, telling us not to worry and that they'll pay for as much as they can. In my bubble of adulthood away from the family home, it looks like they're on the up and up. They're selling our old house to the couple we bought the condo from and are up-grading to a mansion on a river thirty minutes north. I see the struggle they're going through to get the new house, but in my naïveté, figure they wouldn't be buying it if they couldn't afford it. As far as I know, things are getting better for everyone.

At the office, I'm caught drawing a picture of a co-worker's son for a birthday card in a simple paint program. Much to my surprise, instead of putting my job at risk, it opens up new opportunities. I'm soon asked to help with newsletters and assist in designing marketing pieces. It's the boost of confidence that I never knew I needed.

The realtor selling my parents the mansion says that her husband's a creative director at a fancy ad agency in the city. I call him, and he brings me in to review my portfolio of random renderings.

"Did you use Photoshop for these?" he asks.

"What's Photoshop?" I ask. "I only have MacPaint."

Familiar with the program, he replies in disbelief, "So you didn't use any layers? These were each done in one go?"

Embarrassed for my lack of technology, I say, "Yeah. Well, I started over a few times."

"If this is what you can do with that limited software, there's no telling what you could do with some training," he tells me. "How would you feel about starting in a non-creative position here to get your foot in the door and start learning? Then, when you're ready, you can move into the creative stuff. You're going to make a lot of money some-day," he says smugly, inspiring confidence.

I look past him to the panoramic view of Boston from his corner office on the fortieth floor. I look out into the hallway to see stylishly dressed people instead of drab business drones. And then I look into his eyes and say, "That would be fantastic. Oh my God. I'd love to."

I'm hired on the spot. I negotiate five thousand dollars more than I was getting and am beaming with hope for my-self for the first time—maybe ever. I'm going to get paid to work someplace exciting with cool people. I have an actual career path. It almost seems too good to be true.

James is thrilled for me, but his mother is skeptical. She used to tell me that I needed a better career, and now that I'm getting one, she's worried that I won't have enough time to cater to her son. I can do nothing right for this woman. And the more I become empowered by people at work, the less I care about her and what she thinks. Of course, she doesn't like that either.

* * *

One evening, before James is home from work, I decide to try Luke's old number. To my surprise, he answers, and I realize I don't know what to say.

"Hey, remember me?" I tease.

"Millie—Hi, how are you doing?"

"Well, I guess I'm getting married," I tell him.

"You guess?" he asks.

"I mean—I am," I say nervously. "I don't know why I

called," I confess. "You just popped into my mind, and I thought I'd try you. So how are things with you?"

"Pretty good," he says. "Work is good. I'm dating someone."

"Is it serious?" I say.

"Yeah," he says.

"Do you think you guys will get married?"

"Hmmm, probably," he says, as if just considering it.

"Well, that's great. I'm glad you're happy."

"I'm glad you're happy too," he says. "You still in insurance?"

"God no," I say with relief. "I'm working in an ad agency now, training to be a designer. It just sort of fell into place. I mean—I work hard and long hours. But it's kind of awesome."

"That's really cool," he says sincerely.

Oh, how I've missed his sincerity.

"Yeah," I say, not knowing what else to say. "Well, sorry for the weird call, but it was nice to catch up."

"Thanks for calling," he says politely. "And congrats on your engagement."

"Oh, thanks," I say. "Good luck with your girlfriend."

"Thanks."

"Bye, Luke."

"Later, Millie."

I lie back on the bed with a smile, thinking of Luke. Sweet Luke. I hope his girlfriend is wonderful.

THE SHOW MUST GO ON

The wedding feels like a hijacking and two days before, I phone my mother in tears. James and I are fighting. I've thrown my ring at him. I want to call it all off but am afraid of all the backlash it'll cause with partial refunds, gift returns, and the dreaded gossip. She says it has to be my decision and mine alone, but I don't think she understands how badly I need steering. In the end, I decide it's easier to give it a shot than to deal with everything right this minute.

The day itself is such a shame because it would be beautiful if I could just be there. Instead, like I did through most of my childhood, I let my spirit hover over my body and just watch myself do the things I know will make others happy.

I was given the advice to stand in the corner of the room at some point in the night and observe it all for future memory. I do this, and it doesn't feel like how it's intended. I could leave and no one would be the wiser. But of course, I don't.

Since the big day, I've been developing some strange behaviors at home. When food is delivered to our door, I hide in the other room so the delivery guy doesn't see me. James doesn't really get it, and I can't say that I do either. There's just something that feels unsettling to me about strangers seeing me here and like this.

I've also taken to the dry bathtub. I suppose in a way that it's just moving on from the little closet in my old room. I need a retreat for privacy away from James and to be in my own thoughts. I need to get away from this feeling of being a middle-aged housewife. I lock the door, and this freaks James out.

"I don't see why you have to be in there," he says from the outside.

"I just need some time to myself, James. Can you please just leave me alone?"

"But what did I do? I'm quiet," he says.

Eventually he gives up and goes back to watching sports or playing video games. And I get back to writing in my little journal or just gazing up at the ceiling.

I'm so frustrated. I can feel so much heat swirling around in my chest, and I don't understand why. I finally have a cool job, I own a condo, and I'm married to someone who loves things about me that I don't even like. On paper, I have no right to be unhappy. But there it is, in my chest, steaming out through my eyes.

Little things that always bothered me about James start to inflate. Sure, he objectifies every attractive woman that comes on television, but every guy I know does that. He dissects how they look as if each body part should be graded

and every woman should be scored. It makes me feel insecure. All of my guy friends do the same, and James assures
me that if guys say they don't, they're lying. Every man as-
sesses each woman based on whether or not they'd sleep
with her, and that's just how it is. So that means that I'm
actually the problem and need learn to live in the reality of a
man's world.

I tell James that I don't get how he can love me so
much yet have such a high sexual response from looking at
so many other women. He tells me that love is different
from sex. He won't cheat on me, but that doesn't mean he
can't pretend in his head that he could.

It's true—I do have a lot tangled up in my head about
love and sex. Love in itself is hard enough. Ever since sex
came into the mix, it only got more complicated.

There are times when I allow myself to get high or
drunk and have sex with James, only to burst into uncon-
trollable tears halfway through. In these times, he is patient,
kind, and loving. He wants to help, but neither of us knows
where to begin. Things are so messed up inside now. Sex
feels good only if I'm emotionally numbed. And even then,
sometimes the crying fits happen.

I think back to Jared up in Maine and how he used to
cry. At least he was able to wait until we finished. What is it
that fucks us all up?

I'm married now, all painted white. I'm not dirty for
having sex. It's what married people do.

All that talk about waiting for marriage—as if marriage
is when sex is best. Oddly enough, I liked sex a lot more
before I was married—before *we* were married. How can a
simple piece of paper have so much power in the bedroom?

I keep hiding away in the bathtub with the door locked, and James keeps being James. I start taking art classes at Mass Art because my job will pay for most of it, so long as it doesn't interfere with my work. I let it cut into my home life because that seems to be the only place I'm unhappy.

At art school, everyone here is so serious because they're paying for it—likely both financially and with valuable time. It's nice being around people who offer different ways of approaching everything and want to hear what I think about things. It's here where I'm told that I have visual intuition. It's refreshing to be seen for things I can do or just know. It's a great contrast to listening to James and everyone else marveling over the way women are supposed to look and act.

In all fairness to James, he could never be prouder. He boasts about me to everyone he can. He thinks I'm talented and smart and so many things that I'm not so sure about. It's a little awkward but sweet because I know that he means it.

But I can't converse with James about art or much else. It's similar to how I try to follow his sports teams, but something's just missing: genuine appreciation.

The more I grow at school and at work, the more I notice James standing still. He has a job selling construction supplies to contractors all day and only talks about sports, boobs, and classic rock history. I tried to get into his interests, play the part best I can, but at games and at shows I'm an obvious fraud.

One of the perks of working in a big ad agency is we're always given chances to win tickets to events. I surprise James with tickets to see *Page and Plant* at Great Woods, and he's out of control ecstatic.

We're making our way to the eleventh row, center stage, a little high and with a couple of beers each. I'm not smart enough to foresee that we might run into coworkers who also scored tickets. Lo and behold, our company's CFO stands beaming down at us.

To the best of my abilities, I introduce him to James. And then James being James decides to free up one hand by holding his other beer with his teeth. He holds his hand out to shake the CFO's hand, to my horror, then takes the beer back in his hand and starts playing fan boy with the CFO who is there with his son.

At holiday parties and company outings where spouses are invited, I bring James along to share in the luxury. Things always start out fine, but he finds a way to get ahead of himself every time. When a coworker asks how we met, he tells them proudly about how he picked me up at the car wash and that it's been "magic ever since." I am horrified and then guilt-ridden for feeling horrified. And these are the good times.

After another company outing, we're trying to find a party. James punches the car ceiling and bangs on the steering wheel because he can't find the address. My coworkers in the car behind us clearly see him, and I sink in my seat, telling him we'll go home.

His physical outbursts are nothing new. When we met, he had several holes in the wall of his parents' house to repair before we moved into the condo. Helping him with his anger issues is a priority of mine, but I don't seem to be of much help. My telling him to control his anger only fuels him. A few years in, nothing has changed.

One night he actually hits me with his hand full of pizza, right across the face. I lock myself in the bathroom as he slams cabinets and drawers—angry with himself for what he's done. I hear him sweeping things off tabletops with his arms, and things crash to the floor. I smoke nearly three bowls of weed in the tub.

When he's sorry, I always know he means it, but I don't believe he'll never do it again. I assign him to choose a book to read from a woman's perspective about something non-sexual. I want him to see women as people with goals and feelings rather than things just for men's pleasure. And then I tell him my final step is to have his parents over for him to confess what he'd done so that he'll finally take it seriously.

Sitting in our tiny living room in Boston, since we'd sold our condo for me to be closer to work, I pour them each a glass of wine. I tell them that James has something to say and can tell from their faces that they expect the worst.

When he won't say the words, I do. "James hit me," I say, and his mother downs her entire glass of wine.

I'm not quite sure what I expected, but it definitely wasn't what happens next. Both his mother and father wag their disgust at him. They say they always told him his temper would get him in trouble and that they always said he needs to learn to calm down.

I cut in and say, "My condition for staying with James is that he goes to therapy."

"There's nothing wrong with him but his stubborn temper," bites his father. "He needs to learn to be a man. A man never hits a woman. I taught him that."

As they continue to shout proof at how none of this is their fault, I sink into a deeper layer of despair. I realize where James' anger comes from now, but he doesn't, and his parents want to wash their hands of it. I see the long road before me, stretching out so far that I can't believe I'm only in my early twenties. My side of the room starts to sink into a pit as the voices grow further into the distance.

My ventures into the dry bathtub come with a new tool. It used to be just me and the weed on a pillow with a pen and notebook. Now I take in a little penknife I bought for school.

I don't do much with the knife. It's kind of like a dare, similar to when I stood with the kitchen knife to my belly. I drag the blade across my wrist to make marks and to feel the sensation but rarely break skin. And if I do, I have wrist cuffs and bracelets to help keep my secret.

When I bring myself to the peak of numbness, I can see that even with all this life that I've lived, I haven't changed much at all at the core. I'm still a little gun with a trigger waiting to be pulled.

MORTALITY

Three and a half years into the marriage, nothing changes but my promotions at work and where we live because of it. I've been making friends at the new agency on the North Shore, and things start to untangle in my head. I begin to see how wrong things are with James and how much is beyond my ability to repair. I'm nearly ready to process the reality of what it'd be like to start over again. And then Jasminn gets sick.

We notice that her belly is beginning to swell, and her behaviors are somewhat off. They say she has diabetes, so we treat her with insulin twice a day. Months later, the vet says it could either be fixable or fatal, but there's no way to tell without an explorative surgery. As I can't fathom not doing all I can for her, we opt for the surgery. I bring her in one morning and promise to retrieve her.

The day seems to drag on, despite craziness at work with two new business pitches and ongoing clients. Being a senior designer now is great because I can easily afford whatever Jasminn needs. All day I tell myself that I'll do whatever it takes for her to survive because I'm not going to give up on her. She was already abandoned twice when both of her last people died. She needs me, and I need her.

The call comes pretty late in the afternoon. The vet tells me I have to make a decision. He's discovered a sizable tumor, and all of her insides are tangled around it. There's no way to remove it. So either I let him not wake her or have him bring her back and try to treat her pain.

All I can think of is my promise to her. *I'll be back to get you later*, I swore repeatedly, as she cried when I left. I can't betray her by not keeping my word, so I tell him that he must bring her back. I lose myself in miraculous stories I find online.

When I have her back in my arms, I can see right away that I made the wrong decision. Tears fill my eyes to see her shaved and broken, belly swollen and unable to enjoy her favorite food. I build her a cardboard box house using her favorite bath mat as the flooring, showering her with love and attention. And every time I look away for a moment, she sneaks back off to the bathtub. I wonder if she learned that from me.

About the fifth time I pull her out of the dry tub and place her on a fluffy spot on the foot of the bed, she looks at me like never before. It's a heart-stopping, fettered gaze that grapples my heart and holds me at attention. She stares into my eyes for so long that I collapse to the floor so my head can be at her level. She's telling me it's time to let her go. But I just can't bear it.

I cry all my tears into her fur, telling her how much I

love her and will help her get better. I tell her it's not fair and I'm sorry. I'm afraid that if I stop talking, it'll be all over. All the while, she continues her efforts to speak to me with those eyes.

When James comes home, he distracts me for what can't be five minutes. When I realize I can't see her, I rush to the bathtub to find her. She's not there. I fly down the staircase and immediately see her stiff body lying on the floor. I run to her, unable to grasp what's before me.

I shout, "James! Jasminn doesn't look good! She doesn't look good at all!"

I try to pat her and tell her it's going to be okay before I realize she's already gone. She came downstairs to die when I wasn't looking, knowing that I couldn't let her go.

I can still feel the strength of the gaze that she fixed upon me. I know that she was telling me it was okay, but I can't help but feel I let her down. When I brought her home, I promised to make up for the loss she'd been through, but I couldn't help keep her alive. If only I hadn't been so busy with work and school to notice her illness before it was too late. If only I hadn't put her through that surgery. If only I hadn't made the vet wake her up. I did everything wrong, and I can't let it go.

The following weeks are dreadful, and everything everyone says is trite. I don't want to hear it. They don't know how special she was to me, my little adopted baby girl. They don't know how at fault I am for neglecting her. They say things that are supposed to release me from the guilt, but I don't buy any of their cheap tickets out. My Jasminn, the most beautiful being, is gone.

James and I stop fighting while we grieve, and I warily

believe we might be able to get through this together. After a few months, we start visiting shelters and end up taking sister cats home. We call the striped one Amber and the calico one Skyler and focus on giving them a beautiful life. It even goes well for a while.

James starts seeing a new doctor. He takes meds for his anxiety, stops the meds, and is quickly back to punching walls with paranoia.

We live in a townhouse complex with shared laundry facilities. One night he finds men's underwear in the basket that he brings home. Rather than accept that they belong to someone else in the complex, he is certain that it's proof I've been cheating on him. His wheels begin to turn, painting me into an adulteress feigning late nights at the office to go behind his back.

Tonight he won't listen to reason, and just the sound of my voice irritates him. In a fit, he bends down and throws the entire bed into the air. It crashes down with a thundering bang, and little Amber scurries off, barely missing being crushed.

"That's it!" I declare loudly, full of fire. "I give up! I'm leaving you! I want a divorce! It's bad enough that you hit me, but now you put our babies in danger! You could've killed either one of them!"

"I'm sorry, I didn't know she was there," he says.

"Because you don't care about anything when you're in one of your moods! I've given you so many chances, but this is really it. I can't take this anymore!"

I run out of the room, looking for Amber with tears in my eyes. My heart is racing from the pure adrenaline it took to yell like that. I don't like who being with James makes me. I don't like to yell. And I certainly won't bear these close calls from James's anger. I gave him so much time and everything I could—so much that I haven't been able to work out my own problems.

I cradle Amber in my arms, rocking her back and forth, feeling both terrified and exhilarated at once.

ROZ

Once the decision is made, I am solid with it. James doesn't seem to believe I mean it, and I suppose I'm a little to blame for that. I've come close in the past but never quite this far. While I tried to give him and us a chance, I've enabled his behavior by standing by him.

James was the one who was supposed to cure me of being a tarnished girl. He was supposed to be my savior from being a reckless slut. Life was supposed to be fixed by James, but all he did was make things worse. I even tolerated his misogynist ways to a point. I think he loved me, but for me it was never really love. It was always about the need to be loved and be fixed, and I'm sorry that it took me so long to learn it.

Like people said, I was too young. I didn't know what I was doing. I will take all the criticism that comes my way now. At least I know in my heart that I tried, despite my uncertainty at the start. And with any hope, the two of us will leave this union, better and wiser people. I won't wait until someone gets really hurt.

I start to tell family and coworkers and everyone's shocked. I'd kept it all to myself, not wanting to burden anyone with my problems. Nobody tells me I should give it another chance. Many say they never understood our relationship to begin with but wanted me to be happy.

It's at this point, with the word *happy* being thrown around so much, that I realize I don't really understand what it means. Of course I know the basic definition of happy, but I can't say with any certainty any time in my life that I know I was actually *happy*. I've had happy moments and occasions, for sure. But events aren't a state of being. Are they?

Some say life is only a series of events, and we must find our own ways to be happy despite them. And that might be the craziest thing I've ever twisted my mind around. To me, events are what trigger my moods. How can one live in a happy or sad state despite everything going on around them?

There's this girl Roslyn I've been hanging out with lately. She's a cute and delightfully strong-minded, outspoken account exec. We used to work together. She's not afraid to break social or sexual standards, and I love that about her. As I teeter on this new transition of singledom, it feels good to be around people who represent more of what I'd like to be rather than what I've been.

Roslyn and I smoke weed on the couch of my new apartment with the lights off and candles burning. We laugh at the cats chasing shadows on the wall, and I listen to her latest dating adventures. In this new friendship with someone who doesn't have any preconceived notions of who I am or am supposed to be, I find freedom; I find happiness.

When we go out dancing, we talk for an hour on the phone beforehand to discuss what to wear.

"The object of the night is to have fun," I tell her, with a light show going off in my mind.

"Millie, the object of the night is to get laid," she corrects me. We laugh because she really means it.

To be honest, I'm a little afraid of having sex with someone after being with James for so long. Despite Roslyn's—or anyone's—confidence-building, I'm unsure of how guys will react to me. I'm nervous about being naked with someone new. I'm not as tiny as I used to be.

"Girl, you're hot," she assures me. "Plus, there's an entire porn industry based on Asian women. Trust me. You've got nothing to fear."

I hang up the phone and throw on and off clothes for the next half-hour. I try to pretend I think I'm hot for the reflection in the mirror. Laughing at and to myself, I'm never as excited as I am these days and these nights out with Roz.

Roslyn—a pint-sized platinum blonde with huge blue eyes—and myself—an untethered Asian girl with boobs—hit the town something fierce. In our little skirts and platform shoes, we get ushered up the line and make our way to the floor.

I'm sucking down raspberry vodka sodas for insurance. Roz has her arms out and eyes closed, facing the ceiling. I've been dorkishly practicing my moves in the living room at home so I don't make an ass of myself.

I scan the room and try to take in the vibe, loosen up,

and find my zone. And when I do, it's pure magic—a slow unravel of the stress and the worries I've been holding, spinning outward and up. I glance over at Roz, and she's feeling it too. I smile hugely as I fall into my body at last.

We fight off men throughout the night, despite our spoken objective on the phone earlier on. Then Roz finds herself a worthy prospect. I don't find mine, but I'm okay with it, just loving my new life on my own. We split a cab, and they drop me off first then carry on to her place. I anticipate her report the next day.

I smoke some more and dance with the kitties until three in the morning. I wake up on my couch, music blasting, and grin about how none of this matters. For the first time in my life, I am truly free. And for the first time, I'm in a state of self-acknowledged happiness.

This natural high attracts all the right people. I'm kicking ass at the new dotcom I work at in the city. The only time I'm ever brought down is when James calls: a reminder that I haven't gotten too far.

James and I share custody of the cats, despite my fear of his anger inadvertently hurting them. I can see how broken he is and can't deny him the cats. I know he loves them, and they love him too, and I decide that he'll likely be extra cautious. The only problem with joint custody is our continued conversations and exchanges.

Painfully awkward is an understatement. I can practically see the tension steam from his ears as he tries so hard to keep cool when he arrives to pick up the cats. He wears things that I used to say I liked. He's been working out so much that it emphasizes the stress in his shoulders. And because of this contrast and our physical separation, I can finally see him clearly. I look at his built-up stature and still see the insecurity in his eyes. I see a wounded child looking for a love that consumes him. I know this feeling firsthand and hate myself for not being able to love him.

I'm always in such a state after he leaves. I find myself in the dry tub again, smoking and strategically cutting. It soothes me to see my own skin break blood. I punish myself for hurting James and for loving my new life without him. And what's worse is my guilt for not wanting to die. I'd grown so accustomed to feeling that suicide was the eventual way out that it's like betraying an old friend.

You can't solve his problems. He's not your problem to solve, I say to myself in the tub. *You need to fix yourself, and he needs to fix himself. It's just how it is. Even if it was love, it wouldn't be enough.*

Once I've either smoked or cut myself numb, I crawl out of the tub and pretend to carry on like a normal person.

BROTHERLY LOVE ²

Call it romanticism for what could have been or just plain stupidity, but I get this idea in my head to write Derek—the hockey player I met in Montréal years ago. I paint him a picture of my new happy life and say I'm just wondering how he's been. I don't expect a reply but am dizzy with excitement when he wants to get together for a drink.

I show up at the bar—a ten-minute walk from my place—head high and legs confident. As he turns his head to catch me grinning toward him, I sit beside him, and we smirk at each other in silence.

"You look nice," he says, eyes all flirt.

"As do you," I say, breathing down on my adrenaline.

We fidget with our coasters a little, and it's clear to us both that the chemistry is still very much there.

He hasn't aged much, but I like what time has given him. There's more certainty in his eyes as he talks about where and who he is now. The way he looks at me as I tell him my story shows a hint of admiration that he doesn't fight to cover.

"I thought you'd land on your feet," he says. "You always had a kind of way about you."

"Thanks," I say, sipping my drink a little on the fast side.

Being in his presence feels so good. I can't help myself from trying to enhance it even further.

"So you live around here?" he says, nodding out to the Back Bay. "This is a nice neighborhood. I work on a lot of condos around here."

"I just live down the street," I say with a grin. "Do you want to see it?"

We finish our drinks in an unspoken rush and giggle our way to my apartment.

Derek's impressed with my place and how my life appears from the outside. We start making out, and he keeps stopping to look at me and marvel, "You're so awesome." I feel on top of the world with him here and wonder to myself if this is how it's supposed to go. Maybe our past selves weren't ready for one another, and all this time was needed for things to be right.

We shower together. I'm uncomfortable being so naked with him, washing off all my makeup and style. We talk, and he washes me a little. It nice to feel cared for this way when I push off my insecurities.

When he leaves, we make it clear we'll see each other again, and it pains me to watch him go.

Being with Derek again spurs me to call my old friend Kellie. She's still with one of his friends and is piqued to hear things are back on with Derek and me. We make plans to meet at a bar that's local to her and that old crew.

I'm sort of met with mixed reactions. Some of the guys are happy to see me, and others are disappointed that I've become more woman than girl. I look different, speak differently, and they're all pretty much the same. They even listen to the same old songs. It's like that whole bar was in a time capsule while I was off getting married and divorced.

Kellie buys my first rum and coke, and my nerves suck it down pretty quickly. I buy us both our seconds while she reintroduces me around the room. There's a somewhat older, dark-haired guy with glasses whose eyes I can feel on me. I ignore it, not wanting to indulge my paranoia, and catch up with everyone's past six years.

We're standing in another room where a band's about to play when I fall to the floor. Well, I don't fall so much as slip down the wall to my ass. Kellie and her friend help me up, and I say I don't know what the hell happened.

As I rise to stand, a face appears in front of my mine and wouldn't you know, it's Damien—Derek's brother. Kellie shows him my hand and says, "Look! No rings!" And it's like I've been released from the zoo, unclamped and uncaged, the way he looks at me.

My eyes open to an unfamiliar room. I spot my clothes folded neatly on the floor. I turn my head to see a shamrock on an arm and panic. I almost scream but then realize that the guy beside me is Damien.

I must've startled him as he stirs and says, "You're awake! How you feelin'?"

I look down to the oversized T-shirt I'm wearing. "I'm confused," I say. "What the hell happened? How did we end up here?"

"You don't remember?" he says. "You were freezing and shaking. I nearly took you to the hospital."

"All night?" I ask, surprised. "I don't get it..."

"Did you take anything aside from alcohol?" he says. "You said you didn't."

"No," I say. And then I picture the strange guy from the bar and remember falling to the floor.

"We thought you were just really drunk, so I took you here. And then you started acting stranger," he says.

"Imagine if you didn't..." I say and shiver from the thought of what might have been.

"Who was that weird older guy at the bar?" I ask Damien.

"What weird guy?" he says.

"There was some guy who seemed out of place. I don't know. It's all hazy."

"Do you think someone might have spiked your drink? I bet someone slipped you a roofie!" Damien says, eyes wide and excited.

"Shit!" I say.

"That makes sense," says Damien, "because you weren't making *any* sense at all."

"Shit," I repeat, looking at the time on my phone. "I've got a presentation this morning. I have to go!"

I call Kellie from traffic telling her what we think may have happened. "There was a time when you had another drink and I didn't," she says. "I thought that was weird since we were sharing rounds."

"This is fucked up," I tell her, "and now I have to go to a really important presentation this morning with the ex-VP of Fox!"

Kellie laughs. "You'll be okay, hon. Call me later."

Myself and three guys—Creative Director, Copywriter, and Account Exec—pile into the CD's little sports car. Even in the front, I feel nauseated as we speed through the city to the client's office. I'm relieved to get out of the car into the fresh air but it's short-lived. I'm quickly ushered indoors to impress the people of power.

As an art director, I have to create an experience that justifies and sells my designs. While I'm not performing at my best, both clients are happy enough to move forward with my direction. I'm relieved that the work makes up for my lack of charm.

Back at the office, I'm tempted to go home sick but am thrown into the next phase of this project. My entire day feels like I'm missing real life going on without me back home.

Who would roofie someone—especially in that bar where most people know each other? Could I have been roofied? Nothing else would make sense.

Who was that strange guy? Was it him? If not, who else might've done it? Was it Damien? Can I trust him? He folded my clothes so neatly... but he didn't take me to the hospital. Could he have been hiding something?

Damien and I make plans to talk more about what happened the other night. While I'm sober and he says he is, I'm not buying it. He starts off nostalgic, showing me the mix tape I made him, reminiscing about when I said goodbye years ago. But then he gets kind of strange.

"You just dropped me for that guy you married," he says. "Like I didn't mean nothin' to you. How would you feel if I told you I didn't care about you? Because I don't."

"Are you trying to upset me, Damien?" I ask, perplexed. "I'm not sure why you're saying this stuff."

And then he switches gears. "The other night you told me you make about a hundred grand a year. Is that true?"

"Yeah, it is," I say, "but I don't know why I would've told you that."

"You spilled your change all over the parking lot. I was getting it for you, and you said to forget it, it didn't matter because you made all that money," he says.

"Well, that's obnoxious," I say, cringing at the thought.

Damien starts telling me this story about how one of his friends killed another one of their friend's mother.

"Oh my God, I think I saw that on the news. I knew the names were familiar. That was him?" I gasp.

"Yeah, he did it and none of us know why. It's fucked everything up for all of us," he says. "Kellie's guy is a prison guard where he's at now. It's like nobody knows nothin' no more."

Being there with him in that room has a paralyzing effect on me. A part of me really wants to go back to my apartment, but something won't let me. So I stay there with Damien as he falls asleep.

"Save us, Millie. Save all of us," he pleads, and fades off.

The next day I realize his brother Derek hasn't called, and I have so much to tell him. I decide to give him a ring.

"Hey, I was wondering how you were," I say.

"I dunno," he says distantly. "I heard you went to see my brother."

"Oh my God, I don't know where to begin," I say, frazzled.

"You don't have to say nothin'," he says, upset.

"No, I do," I say. "Listen, I don't know what happened, but we think some guy spiked my drink the other night at the bar. I went with Kellie, and your brother just happened to be there. He took me home and said he nearly brought me to the hospital." I don't mention that he had sex with me while I was in my state.

"I didn't hear any of this," he says. "What do you mean someone at that bar spiked your drink? We're there all the time—the whole crew. Nobody would've done that."

"Ask your brother," I say, biting my lip. "Something happened. Kellie saw me fall to the floor after two drinks. They were worried, and Damien said he'd take care of me. I just woke up beside him, confused."

"Why wouldn't my brother tell me that?" he says incredulously. "He said you came to his house, and he didn't even want you there."

"What? Derek—I think something's wrong with Damien. Is he using drugs? He didn't seem right," I say. "He was kind of all over the place."

"If you were only at Damien's because you were roofied, then why'd you go back?" he asks.

"So we could talk about what happened," I explain. "I had to leave really abruptly after waking that morning. I had a presentation."

"I dunno," Derek sighs. "I didn't think... Ugh. You know, you're a good person and everything, but I don't have time for this crap."

"But you don't understand," I try to say. "It really wasn't my fault."

"Just be careful, all right? I don't want nothin' to happen to ya."

I let out a meager, "Yep," and we hang up.

ECSTATIC

Losing Derek for the second time isn't easy, and I'm certain it's going to haunt me forever. Then Roslyn calls and says we're past due for another night on the town. I tell her about Derek and Damien, and she's sure she can help me stop worrying about them.

Dressed to kill and with a healthy buzz from the bong, we hit the club with fire in our eyes. We make drinking and dancing our business. Nothing else matters tonight.

My eyes aren't much for scanning the room this time. I'm just happy to *be*. Carelessly dancing with myself, I have no interest in meeting anybody. Now and then Roz and I connect glances and smiles, and it's all I really need.

But as the night nears to an end, I spot this one guy also dancing alone without a care in the world. I point to him, and Roz makes him out to be gay. I'm quickly disheartened, as living in the South End of Boston has a way of making single straight girls feel underappreciated. Instead of giving up, though, I decide to dance his way.

Our eyes lock. I notice he has an eyebrow piercing, and it looks sexy as hell. His eyes are large and deep—like a pool full of passion soaking in themselves. I smirk at him, and he smirks back devilishly. I motion with my finger to call him over. When he nears, I shout in his ear, "Are you gay?"

He says, "What?"

And I repeat, "I said, 'Are you gay?'"

"No!" he says. "Are you?"

"No!" I say, laughing.

"Then why'd you ask if I was?"

"My friend said you might be," I say, shrugging, giving Roz up.

We laugh and continue on dancing. I love the way he moves—so freely and with such confidence. When he looks in my eyes with those big pools of mystery, I can practically feel my heart shift from its spot and melt down to my stomach.

His name is Seamus, and I don't realize until we're in the cab back to my place that he's Irish. I wish he came with subtitles. He has a thick and sloppy Western Irish accent and a velvety voice. I have to get him to slow down to understand him until we start making out hard.

I'm so excited to have him in my apartment that I can hardly contain myself. I just let myself follow him, and we have an incredible time together. We each confess our biggest secrets, and I'm happy with the way he handles my divorce and *The Incident*.

Then something happens. We're lying there together when a sharp, stabbing pain gets a hold of my stomach. I excuse myself for not feeling well and lock myself in the bathroom. And because the bathroom is so close to the bedroom, my body or brain won't allow me to do whatever it is I need to do. I just sit here clenched up in a ball, biting my knees, wishing the pain would end.

I must've been here for hours, as Seamus even knocks on the door twice to see if I'm okay. I force myself out of the bathroom a few times and try to pretend I'm not in excruciating pain. As much as I want to stay in bed with Seamus forever, I'm delighted when he leaves.

With the apartment free to myself again, I realize that my body can't do anything at all. I take fistfuls of painkillers—Tylenol and Ibuprofen—until I feel somewhat functional. I make an appointment with a doctor right away.

As it turns out, I have an ulcer. I'm not supposed to drink at all while it heals and honestly, I don't know how I'll manage. Drinking socially has become my release. I can't go out to bars and not drink. I need it for my nerves.

I'm telling Roslyn about my recent events, and she starts telling me about how ecstasy is where it's at. She's tried it a couple times and swears that it's better than drinking. I tell her I want to get *The Book of E* and do some research.

I breeze through the book in a couple of days. I read stories and facts online. I learn all the things to do and not do and how to manage my body when on it.

The thing that worries me about E is that it's a hard drug. I was once a peer leader in middle school, for fuck's sake. I was told that hard drugs were too big of a risk and how quickly one could lose everything—even life. But I guess I decide it's a risk I'm willing to take to experience how it feels to be ecstatic.

Another shared, past coworker friend of ours tells Roz that he can get us some E. I like this guy. I think we both had little crushes on one another at different times, but I was married and all back then.

Roz and I cab it to Zachary's place in Beacon Hill. We talk about the night, and he decides he'll come with us. I'm supposed to meet Seamus at the club later on. That in itself has me flying pretty high, and we haven't even popped the pills yet.

We give each other code words in case we need anything out in the big bad world. The two of them prepare me for what it'll be like coming up, when I'm high, and coming down.

"If you're starting to feel sick, just tell us," they say. "But try to relax. You're gonna love it!"

Roz and I take half a pill each to start, and Zach swallows one whole. We get in the cab and head into Lansdowne. I'm slightly panicked that I'm coming up every five minutes and what could happen if the pills are bad.

At the club, we get waters, and I spot Seamus dancing in the middle of the floor. From that moment on, I know everything will be fine.

I join Seamus and escape into a rock n' roll blitz. We hardly speak. We don't need to. Everything that's happening to us and all around us is more than enough.

Now and then I seek out Roslyn to *squee!* into her face and vibe off one another. I can tell she's feeling good. I look over to Zach in the corner and see he's feeling pretty good too. I drag us all together, and we spin miles over how good each of us feels. We decide we should keep it going and take another.

We bring Seamus back to Zach's place and light some candles up on his roof deck. We smoke a little weed to help ease off the E. It must be the best night of my life.

When Zach and Roz chat to themselves, Seamus marvels at my legs and my choice of footwear. He wants to know about the tattoo on my leg, and I tell him a little about my cat Jasminn. We talk about music and life until the sun starts to rise. By then, we're all exhausted and decide it's best to retire to our own comfy beds.

I sleep wonderfully for about four hours and wake up feeling surprisingly fresh and full of life. I'm not hungover like after a night on booze. Possibilities in the world feel endless. In fact, I decide to seek out a tattoo parlor to get my navel pierced.

It's amazing how the thrill of trying new things reminds us how much more life has to offer. It's easy to get dulled into a stage of existence that barely resembles what living really means. Adults don't seem to explore enough. They think wearing a wild tie is living.

AMERICAN DREAMERS

Seamus and I lie on our sides facing each other about a foot apart. Candles are lit around the room, and he's gently caressing my arm.

"I think I'm falling in love with you," he says, and gasps slightly inward.

My body feels like it's floating. Together, we levitate toward the ceiling.

"I think I am too," I say carefully.

It's not that I'm nervous since he said it first, but it's like I'm afraid to break the moment by speaking. Everything is too perfect with him.

"I think you're my soul mate," he says. "I never believed there'd be a girl like you, but here you are."

My whole being is fuzzy from the words that he speaks. We lie together, dancing hands above bodies, crossing limbs like kaleidoscopes, fading in and out of reality.

The two of us spend a lot of time in hysterics, laughing

at anything and everything. We love all the same music, food, movies, and books. It's pretty hard to believe.

"We have everything, you and me," he says. "We can go out all smart for a nice dinner and wine, enjoy a good rock show, and have earth-shattering sex. We've got it all, baby."

Falling for Seamus has this undeniable and very visceral effect on me. I want to spend all my money on him. We run away together on weekends and always enjoy each other's company. I find myself no longer interested in my job or anything besides being with him.

"I'm jealous of your relationship," says Roz.

"Awe, don't be," I say.

"It's just that you guys like each other so much. I don't know what that feels like," she says.

I think about it and smile, saying, "We're pretty lucky."

Roslyn just sighs, and I feel for her. Before I met Seamus I was right there with her, not believing in anything this powerful. I was a cynic. If this was her, I guess I'd be a little jealous too, wishing I could feel what it's like to be in it.

Paradise with Seamus lasts a good few months. He moves in around month three or four, but it feels like we've known each other all our lives—maybe even in past lives. Anything feels possible all of a sudden. I start writing my first novel, and we decide to start looking for a dog.

I quit my job and decide to freelance, which really means working part-time so that I can write as much as possible. I'm tired of helping rich companies I don't care about make more money. Seamus believes in my writing and thinks I have what it takes to make it happen. And because everything's all going so goddamned well, of course something fucks it up.

It starts off slowly enough. Seamus is waiting in the pub to get paid on a Friday and forgets to tell me. Or he thinks that he will and time gets the best of him. Whatever gets the best of him, it's not me because he comes home drunk and argumentative.

At first I try to be cool about it. I say, "I don't want to interfere with your fun. Just call me and tell me you're held up so I don't keep reheating dinner and waiting." He seems to think that's a good idea. Until it happens again.

The first time I witness his mood swing, I'm so caught off-guard that it hits me right dead on the nose. When it keeps happening, I realize I'm totally losing it because this incredibly open and loving guy cannot be the crazy one, right? This man that I feel so much for, who can feel so much with me, can't be the bad guy.

I'm delicate with Seamus now, which makes things a lot less fun. I never know when his warm, loving face is going to turn around and spit in mine. I can't predict when he'll suddenly become insecure or offended and disappear for the night.

When things are good, it's nothing short of magic—the connection we have. There are no words to describe the magnitude of energy transferring between us. But when they're not good, well, they're suicide begging at your feet.

Seamus, like me, is a dreamer. He's always got plans on how we can design our life together. Swung upside down and over his shoulder on the stick that he holds, I follow him everywhere. We get the most beautiful dog, move to JP by the parks, and when that's not good enough, to Key West. I'll write my novel, and he'll start a sailing charter.

We'll take the dog out to the sea and cater to wonderful artists and writers and explorers. We'll eat the best vegetarian
fare and drink the finest of wines. Every night we'll eat dessert and find a rock show. I don't even care much for dessert, but when Seamus orders it, I can't deny the anticipation in his smile coaxing me to never hold back.

Things never go as planned, though, as they annoyingly
say. Down in Key West, that thing that always happened
happens all the time. Seamus flips at the most random
times and runs off hoping that I'll either leave him alone or
follow him, begging. I can never be sure which he wants but
end up chasing him and then going crazy without him—
which translates to scraping my wrists.

When he finally comes home, he's quiet, waiting to riff
off of me, I believe. By then, the raging emotions beating
my chest all night usually leave me too weak to fight. His
absence always resolves in new plans of how we must make
another big change. He wants to try to be as happy as we
once were, and I want that too, more than anything else. I
never know what he's really done while he's gone and a big
part of me doesn't want to.

Our dog is the only promise fulfilled. He's the constant
reminder to smile and that despite all the shit in this ugly,
unstable world, life is pretty amazing. I spend more time
outside taking him places I'd never otherwise visit. He and
Seamus's Irish friend, Owen, come with us down to Key
West to live out the American Dream.

I love this dog Shaunnessy to pieces, but I'm not good
for him. The tumultuousness of my relationship has me
running off into streets in the middle of the night. Sometimes he escapes just to follow. He and Seamus wait out-

side locked bathroom doors begging me to come out. We come home on drugs, patting him while high. He must feel something's wrong. If he were a human baby, we'd have severely damaged the child already.

We try to have fun when we can though. I take him everywhere with me down here. He hates to be left alone. He's had separation anxiety from the very first week of being ours. When I'm not hostessing or carrying around Jell-O shots, we go swimming and sunbathing together.

The day after another big Seamus disappearance that has Owen and I driving around searching for him, he returns and says we made a mistake and have to move back to Boston. We had everything there and didn't know it, all of our friends, everything but the view. Key West is for shallow plastic people or people who are running away from real life. We don't want to be that, do we? I agree that we don't. It's decided, just like that, and we'll tell Owen about it real soon.

That same day, Seamus goes off to start a new job at a marina. Despite it being on the direct path to his dream job, I imagine our new plans will make it short-lived. Little do I know just how short.

I get a phone call a few hours later. It's him. He says, "Listen to me very carefully. I don't have long. I'm at a detention center in Miami, and I'm being deported. Call my mother and get her to transfer you money. I have to pay for my own ticket home or else stay here in jail."

"What? What happened? Oh my God," I say, stunned.

"I can't really get into it now. Some guy at the marina gave me up—said I'm here undocumented. They grabbed me as I was about to go in," he says hurriedly.

"What are we supposed to do—me and Shaunners," I ask, "and Owen? He's only here because of you. Now he's got to go back home to Ireland? He can't stay here with no one."

"What will you do?" asks Seamus.

"I'm coming with you," I say. "I'll find a way to bring Shaunnessy to my parents' house and fly over to you."

"God love ya," he says. "You're the best girl. I'll make it up to ya in spades. All of this. Promise. I have to go."

"I'll call your mother," I say. "Love you."

"Same as that," he says, and hangs up.

TO GREENER PASTURES

For all the shit I've been through with my family, they rise to the occasion of my failure. My dad sends (slightly less) Angry Brother down with a couple others and a truck. We pack everything and spend a couple of days driving straight back to Boston. I'm given help toward getting Owen and me to Ireland and the promise of having my boy, Shaunnessy, well cared for.

Saying goodbye to Shaunners breaks my heart. Not only has he lost his father figure so abruptly, but now the person he's been attached to at the hip is leaving him too. He has other dogs and ten acres of land to explore and a lot of people who love him though. I wasn't so good for him anyway. He'll be okay, I hope. It's what's best for now.

Ireland is amazing. I'm welcomed with open arms. A room is made up for Seamus and me to share—which is a big deal in this very Catholic home. His mother is grateful to me for helping her son out of the detention center. But her kindness and willingness to accommodate me has this very lapsed Catholic feeling guilty.

Seamus's mother and father are as ignorant as they are sweet when it comes to our real relationship. At first we're the golden couple, shown off at their own pub. Everyone is so kind and seemingly genuine to me. They want to know all about me. And there I'd been, fearful of prejudice against my Asian appearance.

We live with Seamus's family in a quaint village for a few months. I spend my days working on small freelance projects online, spending a fortune on bandwidth, as Ireland isn't yet on broadband. In the meantime, I'm feverishly writing my new novel and have query letters out to literary agents in New York. I spend close to everything I've got saved photocopying and posting things back to the States.

Seamus and I are returning from town one afternoon when his mother greets us outside excitedly.

"Has it finally happened?" says Seamus, before she can say a word.

"What," says his mother, puzzled.

"Are they coming with the white coats? Millie, run!" he says, as if it's a totally normal thing to say.

His mom laughs, familiar with her son's offbeat wit. "Millie—an agent called and said he wants your whole book!"

"Really?" I say, with the wind knocked out of me.

"He called at half-two and asked for you to call him back. I took down the number," she says proudly.

Now, I'm thrilled with this news, obviously, but I'm not without my concerns. My novel, *Mourning Malyssa*, depicts a glamorized version of Seamus and me. It boasts graphic sex and drug use, suicide, and murder—mostly fiction, of course, but the characters take after us. If this book's a success, I can't have this sweet lady learn the truth about whom she's hosting. When treated as if you're a good person, you shift who you want to be in your mind. I'm just getting comfortable with this version of myself.

But as a writer, you're supposed to write without fear in order to speak the truth. I don't know if people are ready to handle the truth—not the ones who think they know me, at least. I wrote this novel as if no one would read it. Do I really want it published now?

Mitchell, the agent, says he's pretty confident that he can sell it. He believes in it and says it has huge potential. He says there aren't many female writers with strong voices and stories like mine. He's sending the contracts to sign and will get straight to work.

We all celebrate over at the pub. My stomach's in knots with excitement and anxiety. Seamus's friends join us from Galway and hit the pints with a little more rigor than what's been fairly moderate since we arrived.

I must've been in denial or floating on a thin layer of hope until now. Seamus's mother sees when it happens this time—the switch from good son to demon. She tells me we should go home and leave them to it, so I do. I sit on the edge of the bed, scribbling furiously into a journal.

I feel even more alone now, in his country, when he changes like this. But at least I have someone else to confirm that what's happening with him isn't about me.

Seamus's mother comes to check in on me and sees the red in my eyes. I fight hard to hold back, but the gentle concern in her face cripples me helplessly with tears.

She wants to know if this has happened before then tells me to run while I still have the chance. She loves Seamus, of course, but says I deserve better than what he can give. She sits there and lets me cry on her shoulder while assuring me that it's not my fault.

Not long after she's gone, Seamus walks in stone-faced, asking what the "feck's" wrong with me. He tells me that I disgust him, that I'm lower than dirt, and how he can't believe he was fooled by who he thought that I was.

"Why are you doing this, Seamus?" I ask, and I beg for what I know I can't have. He walks away and never returns that night.

The next morning, I come out of the shower to find Seamus sitting with my journal.

"What have I done?" he asks with watery eyes. "Please, tell me what I've done to make you feel the way you say you do in this book."

"Where were you?" I ask with both anger and relief.

"I slept upstairs in Laura's old room. I woke up there, I mean. I don't remember anything," he says, and I believe him.

"Seamus, you've really done it this time. Your mother knows," I say.

"How does she know?" he says.

"She saw you. And then she came in when I was crying," I say. "You said awful things to me. And you were being so crass and rude at the pub!"

"I'm so sorry," he says. "Please forgive me. I'll do anything to make it up to you."

Seamus opens up to his mother, and the two of them

decide he has a problem with alcohol. She asks me what I think and I say, "I don't know. I think the alcohol has a problem with him." We both keep an eye on him with false hope that we have any control at all.

Seamus and I eventually leave the family house to live in Galway. With Galway, it's love at first sight. I'm in awe of the bridges over the river, the swans, the ocean, and the feel of the stones under my feet—even if they do twist my ankles. I don't even mind the rain in Galway or the scientific nature of rain meaning worms.

We get a place with one of Seamus's brothers and another friend on Nun's Island. All the apartments—*flats*—come furnished in this country, making it so much easier for young adults to get on. Seamus gets a construction job, and I keep on writing, waiting for good news from New York.

Excited about my new novel in progress, *Waiting for the Music*, I make the mistake of sharing its unfinished version with my agent. He sees its promise too and thinks it could be an easier breakthrough for me. Soon, he's involved in my writing process, which throws everything off a bit, as I'm no longer guided by my own imagination but his thoughts as well.

In the meantime, rejection letters are pouring in from publishers saying what we know—gratuitous sex and drug use, *blah blah blah*. Mitchell says it's all part of the process. They're positive rejections, as they all love my style but just can't get behind the content. He says they "don't get it" and that's fine because we only need the one who does.

In Galway we can get high again, go dancing, and have more sex. There's a decent underground culture here. We can pretty much get anything we need. There's this "Death Disco" night with big DJs and the promise of Shane MacGowan.

Speaking of which, that's another thing with Seamus. I'm the fiction writer, but he has this instinct to tell tall tales. He told me and several others that he used to play with the band *The Pogues*. His friend Owen and some others confronted him with his fibs, yet he continues to swear by his stories.

"Why do you do that, Seamus? People already think you're cool. You don't have to make up lies," I say.

I can see Seamus thinking for a moment. Then he says, "It's low self-esteem."

And with that kind of honesty, there's nothing much to add.

SLEEPING
WITH THE KNIFE

The crying spell happened again. I came to with a throbbing sore face and no recollection of what happened. Seamus says I was inconsolable and unable to respond—I was crying that hard.

"I don't cry," I tell him.

"Coulda feckin' fooled me," he says, but there's concern in his eyes. "Something's wrong witcha," he sighs, shaking his head.

If it was perfect, it'd be perfect. I never thought I would love Ireland so much. I'm living my dream, writing novels with a secured agent in a beautiful country that's foreign but welcoming. There's no end to the beauty in the people, the animals, the culture and countryside. Yet I find myself going to sleep with a knife under my pillow, thinking that if Seamus hurts me again, I'll give him a final lasting memory as he wakes up beside my dead body.

On my birthday he spends the day out at the pub with the lads while I wait impatiently for him. He was supposed to just pop in for a check. I dress to the nines for dinner and dancing, applying more jewelry and makeup as times goes on. When he finally shows, he declares he's too tired to celebrate with me after drinking all day. It doesn't matter that I'm a stranger with no friends of my own in this country. It doesn't matter that I left everyone and everything at home for him. This man, who is so capable of feeling so much for others, blocks me out, and I just can't take it.

It's in the waiting that I really unravel. It's the in-betweens of things that I just can't handle. It's the worrying and the wondering if I'm going to be returned to or abandoned forever. The feeling is so intense and somewhat reminiscent of something that I can only attribute to being left by my birth mother. It runs deep and cuts upward inside me. My chest aches from the drop of unlove.

As I wait, I negotiate with myself the best way to be understood. I want him to know that he's killing me as he lies beside me, a vacant shell. I want him to see what he's done to me since nothing I say makes him understand. And then I become angry with him and defiant, not wanting to let him win when I'm on the verge of being published.

When I tell him the motive behind the knife under the pillow, he doesn't show concern for me. Instead, he is worried that I'm framing my own death on him. He's worried about his own life.

I leave Ireland and Seamus and return to America where my dog is waiting for me. I have nothing at all to support myself with. I've burnt so many bridges with work by becoming geographically unreliable. Before I met Seamus, it seemed I had it all. Much bitterness swirls inside me, and I just want to cut all of it out.

I know that I can't blame him. Despite how much he let me down and broke promises, I'm the one who believed him. I knew the odds but went against them, refusing to accept the truth.

When it comes to Seamus, my distance always makes his heart fonder. Every time I leave, he always makes it his mission to get me back. He reports of all the people who miss me dearly, how well he's doing, and how much he's learned in my absence. But this time is different, I tell him.

Temporarily living in my parents' house, a house that I never lived in, feels bittersweet. Once again, I have failed. I try to comfort myself by thinking that at least I'm on a path with my writing, and at least I have all the dogs and cats here to help heal my heart.

Shaunnessy couldn't be happier to have me home. I watch him run with the big dogs, marveling at how much he's grown. But I can't help but worry about him missing Seamus. I wish he knew that it wasn't that he was not loved.

Seamus's friend Owen left a guitar here with the quiet brother. I ask him to teach me some chords. He shows me a couple each week, and I'm determined to break my fingers in to make it sound right.

With the piano, all you have to do is push the keys down. Guitar strings will bear down on nerves you never knew you had, making you bleed for the sound. And so it is fitting for me at this time.

The youngest brother is still just a kid, but he's somewhat of a child prodigy on the drums. He has a kit in his bedroom. When the calluses on my fingers are hard enough, we play music together. I start writing songs again—mostly about suicide and Seamus—but despite the subjects, I love it.

A month later it's Christmas, and the quiet brother gets me in the sibling grab. And what does he buy me? Nothing other than my very first electric guitar. It's so much easier on my fingers and to wear. I nearly throw him in the air with excitement and thank him for the best present ever.

This musician, ex-coworker friend of mine tells me about power chords, and I become all about them. I've never been one to want to master an instrument, so much as command it to express my feelings. I'm writing several songs a week—often several a day. After such a hiatus from music due to *The Incident*, the guitar saves me. I learn that I never needed a guy to save me. All I needed was music back in my life.

Seamus is still trying to win me back. He writes me poems—really bad poems, to be honest, full of spelling errors and clichés. He says he knows how he was wrong and that he's seeing a therapist who's helping him learn to be a better man. He can't believe how he's treated me in the past, he says, and promises things would be different if I'd just return.

I contemplate returning to Seamus, wondering just how much a person can change. He swears I'm his soul mate and that we're meant for each other. But can I ditch my life completely again to join him and his land of broken promises?

One night when I'm high on life, he catches me in a

weak moment. I agree to fly over for a long weekend. We spend it swimming in ecstasy—the drug and the feeling. It's such an intense thing being back together—so intense that we decide to engage to marry. I need to hurry up and get back to him. We'll try Dublin instead because it's where all the good venues are. With my writing and music, his new job and our love, the future is a rock 'n' roll romance.

Leaving Shaunnessy again tears me to shreds. He tries to break through the door to come with me and backs away with sad eyes when he sees that he can't. I wish so hard, more than anything I've ever wished for, that he'll forgive me and know how much I love him. I know he'll continue to be loved and have a good life with the other dogs and the family. I just don't want him to think I'm abandoning him forever. I'm hypersensitive to that.

When Seamus picks me up from the airport and our eyes meet, I instantly feel that it's wrong for me to be here. I don't know why or how, but it's almost like I see things with new definition. Maybe it's just the Dramamine and the flight that has me down and so fatigued, but the spark between us isn't there.

He set us up with a cute flat in Rathmines. I dig the area and being close to Owen again. I meet Owen's friend Seth, a good-looking and very articulate guy. He takes interest in my writing, and we philosophize for hours in pubs. I begin to think this new location might work out after all.

The four of us hit the town fairly often, seeking out a variety of venues: live music, DJ, highbrow, and dive. I'm just feeling comfortable when the next big event in the saga of Millie & Seamus occurs.

Seamus takes off from the club with no warning, so I

follow him out. He won't tell me what's wrong and runs ahead to lock me out of the building. On this cold, rainy night, I spend it crying at the bus stop semi-shielded from the weather. I think to call Owen, but my phone has died. When I have to pee, I squat behind a bush, crying to myself at what I've allowed to happen by giving Seamus another chance. I ring the bell several times, but Seamus doesn't answer. I shiver till the sun comes up.

In the morning, Seamus is gracious enough to buzz me in. I take a hot shower and put on some warm, clean clothes, charge my phone, and walk around on eggshells. I'm afraid to learn what I'm dealing with this time. We avoid each other for hours.

"Why did you do it?" he finally says, emerging from his corner.

"Do what?" I ask, bewildered.

"Don't act like you don't know," he says.

I scan my brain and come up dry. "I honestly have no idea what you're talking about," I say frankly.

"Why did you throw the drink in my face?"

"What?" I say, confused.

"What," he says. "That's all you've got to say?"

"Are you crazy?" I ask.

"I must be," he says, "to have subscribed to this."

"I have zero recollection of throwing anything at you, Seamus," I say. "Don't try to twist this around. You locked me out in the cold rain all night. So now you blame me for something I haven't done? Is apologizing really so bad?"

"You feckin' did it," he says. "I swear on my mother's life."

"Don't swear on anyone's life, Seamus. Especially not

hers!" I say, angered that he'd bring that sweet woman into this.

"Well, you did it. Are you gonna say sorry?" he says, fired up.

"Sorry for something I don't remember doing?" I ask. "Was Owen there? Did Seth see it?"

"Yeah," he says.

"So what did they do when it happened?" I ask.

"They looked at me like the fecker with the drink in his face," he says.

Pissed off, I head back out—with my keys this time. I call Owen and tell him what happened and ask if he saw me do it.

"I didn't see anything like that," he tells me. "We didn't know why you feckers left."

"Listen, Owen, Seamus is adamant that I did this. I don't think I was drunk. Do you remember what I was like? Could I have done this?"

Owen sighs. "Millie, as you know, I've been a right bastard when drunk, which is most of the time. And usually when someone tells me I did something I don't remember, I remember. If you have absolutely no recollection of doing it, it probably didn't happen."

"Do you think I could be crazy?" I ask him. "Seriously, I want to know."

"Without being disloyal to one of my best friends, I'm going to say no. Not from what I've seen," he says.

"Things were really fucked up in Key West, huh," I say to him, looking for validation. "Remember?"

"Of course I remember," he says. "Things were fecking catastrophic. I don't know what makes him like that, to be honest."

"Thank you, Owen," I say, voice breaking as I fight to keep it together. "I don't know what I was thinking coming back here."

"All I can do is wish you luck," he tells me.

Back at home, Seamus is still demanding an apology.

"I'm sorry if I did it," I say. "I don't know why I would do such a thing out of the blue and have no memory of it. But if I did, I'm sorry."

"You did," he says.

"Are you going to apologize for locking me out in the cold?" I ask, looking him in the eye.

"No," he says. "I'm not sorry because you humiliated me. I did what I did because of what you did."

"Are you serious?" I ask him.

And when he says nothing, I punish myself for allowing him back in my life. I take a knife into the bathroom and lock myself in, reacquainting with the drag on the verge of control and losing it.

I decide that this massive pile of shit I've created isn't something I'll ever recover from. There's too much—there's just way too much to fix now. I've ruined my career, traumatized my dog, given up so many things that I've worked hard for. And these books that I write—well, they shouldn't be published, not while I'm alive anyway. It's taking so long for Mitchell to sell them. Maybe they'll have a better chance when I'm dead.

Every time I drag blade across skin, I wonder if I'll ever have the courage to do it for real. I wonder if anyone will ever understand how hard it's always been to be me—even before *The Incident,* the bad marriage, and emotionally abusive boyfriend.

Why has it always been hard to be me? Are some people just cursed from the moment they're born—or before, even? Could I have been a product of rape? Did my birth mother kill herself after having me? Is it woven into my biology, and will it be poetic if I kill myself too?

I've always fantasized about and tried hard to plot the least offensive suicide. I don't want to ruin anyone else's life with my death—especially not a stranger's. Inconsiderate suicides, such as jumping off an overpass into traffic, harm or kill other people. I don't want to die out in the woods and have animals feed off my body and hikers or campers stumble upon the gruesome scene.

I resolve that the perfect suicide would involve me checking into a hotel, ordering room service—such as a steak for the knife—and killing myself in the bathroom. I'll leave a note on the closed bathroom door for the cleaning lady, not to open it but to call 999. That way she won't have to see my dead body. Only paramedics who are used to seeing things like that would find me. That way I could die in peace.

I pack my things, book a hotel, and have Seamus drive me to it under the guise that I'm going home. He's rude to me, of course, which only makes my decision easier.

Sitting on one of the two beds once he's gone, I can't help but realize how different the room looks from what I had pictured in my fantasy. It's a little too nice—not like the dump I nearly killed myself in a couple years ago when I stopped at a place called Hope Valley, ironically enough. Failed suicide after failed suicide floods my head, one after the other. I collapse on my side with my face in my hands and start bawling to myself, feeling like such a coward.

That one voice in my head that sounds most like me starts to speak. It says, *I don't want to die. I never wanted to die. It's just so hard to live.*

I've thought that I wanted to die since I was just a kid—before my mother found it in my diary. Back then I imagined what each person I knew would think about my death, and now I do the same.

No one knows you, says the voice. *No one will understand why you did it. They'll just think you were a selfish person. Why would you want to die without at least first giving people the chance to know who you really are?*

"Who I really am." Who am I, really? I don't know anymore, but I don't fucking like her.

One side of me tries to persuade me to do it, putting everyone else out of their misery. The other side ridicules her, saying quitting is for pussies, and I thought we were supposed to be a badass.

Dying now is only giving in. I have so much to do before I can truly die peacefully.

But the other side keeps saying, in crescendo, *Just do what you came here to do.*

I go into the bathroom to look in the mirror and can't believe how ugly I am. My face is red and swollen, streaked by pitiful tears. I'm not a good-looking girl and never was. I have to tart myself up to look pretty.

My head is spinning so fast that it's hard to think straight. I head back out to the bed and text Seamus.

I write: *Can you come to the hotel?*

He writes: *No. Just go on and feck off will ya?*

I write: *I came here to kill myself. I don't think I can do it. I need you.*

Ten minutes later, he writes: *Jaysus Christ.*

Half an hour after that, Seamus is at the door. I beg him to lie beside me on the bed, but he stays defiantly on the other bed. I turn to the wall and start bawling again. He sighs and comes over to my bed but won't hold me. In my biggest time of need, he always denies me.

The next day he says, "So you haven't booked a flight at all then?"

I shake my head no.

"All right then," he says, grabbing one of my suitcases and dragging it out to his car.

JACKSON & THE GIRL

When I finally leave Seamus and arrive back "home," I make a promise to really move on this time. I start perusing on-line dating sites in bed at night with Shaunnessy's chin on my lap.

Sometimes I hang out the window to smoke a little weed that I got from the quiet brother. It helps buffer the bite of reality of being twenty-nine with no job, no money, and living in a room at my parents' house. It makes it easier to spin my situation creatively too. I highlight that I'm writing novels and songs and just returned from nearly three years abroad.

My dating profile is hidden from the people I don't choose to contact on my own. It shields me from ex-coworkers and ex-boyfriends. Besides, I like the control. For the two days it was public, my self-esteem plummeted from the onslaught of guys who thought they had a chance.

Seamus and I might have had a lot on good days, but we

never had a shared creative endeavor. As I got back into music, I so wished that we could've made music together. This time I decide I will find someone who participates in at least one of my creative interests.

I focus on this guy named Jackson. He writes poetry, also quit his high-paying corporate job, and is taking time to cultivate other interests while working as a part-time bike messenger. He doesn't look like the kind of guy I'd normally be into, and that seems like a good idea.

Jackson and I have a strong physical connection instantaneously. There's something about the need in his eyes that quenches my thirst to feel needed. It's apparent that he took a lot of care honing his bedroom skills. I enjoy benefiting from the failures of his past, and he lavishes in mine. I force myself to expand my sexual fantasies to include ideas that I'm not so sure I want—such as threesomes with other women.

Once I get another freelance gig, I find a room to rent in a house with four other girls. It happens to be just down the street from Jackson. I paint it hot pink and build it into a creative den. I want it to be a place of inspiration, imagining all of the cool things I'll make in it.

I take Shaunnessy down to live with me, but on the first day, he has a seizure. Then I learn that no one in my family wanted to tell me that he started getting seizures while I was gone. I bring him back up to the big house, and he never has a seizure again. So, as much as I wish he could be with me, I realize the best thing I can do for him is to let him stay there and visit periodically.

It's hard to see things for what they are when you're going so far out of your way not to. Jackson and I smoke

weed to enhance our sex life and pop ecstasy to enhance
our emotional connection. We even film ourselves to act
like total rock stars because we don't want to believe we're
anything less. We send poetry to one another, paint can-
vases together, and I'm happy in this cloud for some time.

Aside from our hedonistic ways, Jackson's been hugely
supportive. He encourages my singing, songwriting, painting, and every whim I decide to indulge in. He's breezing
through my first novel, *Mourning Malyssa*, and surprises me
with practical gifts.

Things seem to be going well with us until it comes out
that he's still getting messages from a website people go on
to find sex hookups. He says he was on it for a while before
we met and forgot to leave it. I find that hard to believe and
don't want to trust him. But the thing is, he's just so insis-
tent.

Jackson has been wanting to slide the threesome fantasy into reality. We talk rules as if we might actually do it,
but I share my hesitance with him each time. It seems everywhere we go he makes sure to point out which girls he'd
like to invite into our bed. I want to be more open-minded
about things like this, as it fascinates me. However, watching him objectify all these strangers doesn't feel right. I try
to explain this, but of course he blames me for leading him
on about it instead of hearing what I'm feeling now. I struggle for a reasonable explanation of fantasies in the moment
versus real life plans.

I suppose it shouldn't surprise me to learn that someone so well versed in sex would still watch porn on a regular
basis. I'm said to be both hypocritical and naive to think
being in love and having a rich sex life with one person is

enough.

"All men watch porn and fantasize about sleeping with other women," is what he tells me. "We'd all do it too, if we could without hurting our partners. Don't be such a prude. Besides, you get plenty of good from my sexuality. You shouldn't complain."

No matter how hard I try to be good with that mentality, I still find myself carving lines into my wrist with an exacto blade. I'm confused by his absolute admiration for my brain and my body juxtaposed with such dickishness.

Jackson is a man for whom nothing is ever enough. He wants the world and has the confidence to believe he deserves it. The bulk of me knows and respects all of it, and the rest of me is deeply upset.

In the meantime, I'm still getting texts and voice messages from Seamus that if I don't call him back within a certain span of time, he'll kill himself. My heart shot out of my chest one day when I left my phone off after going to the movies. Thankfully, he didn't go through with it. But this contrast makes what I have with Jackson feel sane.

On the day that I purchase a vintage-looking scooter, I'm riding high on the pit of my being. Jackson rides his bike around with me so that I can get used to driving it. He ends up directing us to the street that his most recent ex-girlfriend lives on. Interestingly enough, we run into her and have an awkward exchange.

Jackson's roommate has been mentioning her a lot around me because, I swear, she's jealous of the time we spend together and wants to stir things up. This has led to conversations about her and my discovery of how he has a hard time letting go of past loves. Nonetheless, I agree to go

with him to a club with her tonight. Some mutual friends'
band is playing.

I have a couple drinks after smoking a little weed. For a
short while, I'm able to enjoy myself there in the midst of
the whole situation. But Jackson is pinned to his ex-
girlfriend's side. Seeing him in such close quarters with her
really burns, despite my knowing what we were getting into.

While shifting my attention to the band, I notice the
attention of a cute taller girl with sandy blonde pigtails and
librarian glasses. I decide to dance with her while they do
whatever they're doing. We step outside so she can have a
smoke, and she invites me back to her place down the
street for some weed.

I remember us skipping down the hill hand-in-hand.
And then I remember waking alone in a strange room on a
bed that has old jeans sewn together into a quilt. I see more
weirdly cut jeans hanging in the open closet and immediately think of *Silence of the Lambs* and that guy who liked to
piece human skin together.

I sit up in shock, taking it all in, and realize that my
clothes are nowhere in sight. I head into the hallway and see
the bathroom door open. I go in to throw up and dry heave
for a while. I steal the towel on the rack to cover myself up.

I can't get over how none of this looks familiar.

There's a big, open room that's jam-packed with junk. I
can't decipher what any of it is. Random pieces of old rusty
equipment and other unrecognizable oddities fill the room
wall-to-wall. At this point I'm certain that whoever brought
me here must be into some crazy shit.

And then out of nowhere, I remember the girl.

There's a closed door in the hallway, and I carefully open

it. I see two guys in bed. One of them stirs, so I shut the door quickly and as quietly as possible.

I stand outside the closed door and think to myself that they didn't look like bad people. Clutching tightly onto my towel, I knock on the door softly.

The one who stirred comes to the door wrapped in a sheet.

I realize that I have no idea what to say.

"Um, I don't know where I am," I tell him. He looks puzzled. "I woke up in that room," I say, pointing behind me.

"He's not even home," he says.

"Well, where is *she*?" I ask, confused.

"*She*?" he says, surprised.

I nod my head, shyly. "I remember a girl."

"Oh," he says, more relaxed now. "I'll take you to her room."

We head down the stairs together. While he knocks on the door, I stand nervously, afraid of what's going to be behind it.

"Come in," I hear a voice sing sweetly.

He opens the door, and she's kneeling topless in underwear, looking pretty. The guy walks away, back up to his room.

Her face quickly transitions from a wide, pretty smile to a frown when she sees my reaction to her.

"I can't find any of my clothes or my purse," I say, shifting my eyes around the room.

"Well, your clothes are over there," she says, pointing. While I throw them on she says, "I don't really remember you having a purse."

I look at her and say, "This is some crazy shit," still not remembering anything. "I woke up naked in a room full of jeans. Do you know why I was there?"

She shakes her head and says, "You just said you had to go to the bathroom and never returned."

I don't ask why she didn't come looking for me. I just moan, "I never leave my purse behind. I have no idea how I'm going to get home now."

Still maintaining a nice demeanor she says, "Well, I can give you a couple of bucks for the T."

"Thanks," I say, scared to look her in the eye.

"Um, I'm going to go in the shower," she says, leaving a couple of dollars on the bed.

Totally dumbfounded about what to do, I hastily scribble my name and number on *The Phoenix* newspaper on the bed.

I grab those two dollars and head out to the street. Nothing looks familiar for about five minutes until I stumble my way to Mass Ave. I ask a stranger how to get to the nearest T stop, and she says I'm equidistant between Central and Harvard. I head toward Harvard, trying to remember Jackson's number but it's no use. It's been programmed into my phone since we met.

When I arrive at Jackson's front door, it's unlocked. I walk up to his room and see a sign on the door. It's written on a white sheet of paper with thin blue rules and reminds me of something I might have done as a child.

YOUR SCOOTER IS IN THE BACK WITH YOUR KEY IN THE IGNITION. YOUR PURSE IS IN THE SEAT. LEAVE!!!!!!!!!!!!!

While I'm relieved that my purse is secure, I know what

I'm getting into is going to be grim. Still, I knock on the door and push it open an inch.

"LEAVE!" he yells, so loudly that he must've woken all four of his roommates. "GO! LEAVE!" He keeps yelling over and over, but I refuse to leave.

"I just need to talk—" I begin, and he hollers over me.

Finally, I walk into his room, close the door behind me, and break down saying, "I have no idea what happened. I just woke up in a strange room."

"You ran off with that girl!" he shouts, full of anger but at least willing to talk.

"I don't even remember," I cry. "I remember we were going to smoke some weed and then the next thing I know, I wake up in the weirdest apartment!"

I explain as much as I remember to Jackson, and he welcomes me into his bed to be held. As I begin to recall little snippets of being naked, making out with the girl, I tell him. He's upset but demands to know everything. And then he takes control of me in bed and bites down hard on my wrist for punishment as he does what he does.

"You're *mine*," he says, pouting like a child. "You didn't even tell me you were going! You just left me sitting in the bar with your stupid purse like a loser! I almost went look-ing for sex on the way home but I stopped myself!"

"I'm sorry," I tell him, as I cry. "I don't know why I did it."

I let him punish and reclaim me because somehow it feels safer than being pushed off on my own.

THE HOMEOPATH & THE SUNBEAM

The longer Jackson and I are together, the more confused about love and relationships I become. On one hand, he has been so good for me. He cares about my past wounds and legitimately wants to help see me through them. But he also makes me feel worthless and devalued with his sexual wants and pushes my boundaries too far. He can never get high enough, so we're never really sober. And mostly, he glamorizes my pain.

Jackson is one of those rare people who grew up without having to tackle any real traumas of his own. He's been there for others close to him who have, but firsthand, he's been fortunate to have it fairly easy. I think a part of him is with me to give his life an edge. But he makes racist jokes and isn't able to believe in the concept of White Power. This bugs me more than anything, really, but I'm not able to articulate my arguments well enough with him.

All of Jackson's issues aside, I'm the one who's going crazy, so I suppose my perspective doesn't carry much weight. Jackson convinces me that it's time to confront my mother with some things that have been bothering me— things I've been too afraid to discuss with her, such as the aftermath of *The Incident* and that time she found my first suicide note.

I call my mother one day and when she picks up, I hold my breath and then break down and say, "Things aren't okay!" And when the dam breaks, all of my intentions fly out the window. It's the first time I've cried in her presence since I've been conscious enough to withhold.

"What's the matter?" she says.

I'm surprised by the calm in her voice. It's funny how I've always maintained that I can't tell her anything bad in case it might hurt her. Just the tone of her voice alone makes it seem as though she's been prepared for this all her life.

Mom to the rescue!

Omitting and inventing some self-protective details, I say, "Weird things are going on. I woke up on the train the other day and had no idea how I got there."

My mother is oddly energized by this story, so my mind skips around. I try to connect some dots for her.

"It's happened before," I tell her. "There was this time that Seamus swore I threw a drink in his face, but I had no recollection of doing so. And another time I was out with Kellie and woke up next to a friend of ours. We all thought someone must've slipped me a roofie."

"But maybe they didn't," she says, more than asks.

"Maybe you just blacked out?"

"I don't know," I say. "Maybe."

This is the longest conversation I remember ever having with my mother without the constant interruptions of someone else. Usually one sibling or another is beeping in on the line or talking to her in person despite her being on the phone.

My mother goes on to tell a long-winded story about one of my relatives—her relatives—who found out she was bipolar. I can't really keep track of the people involved or remember who each of these people are exactly, but she keeps on talking excitedly about them. She keeps talking and talking, and I realize the uninterrupted sound of her voice is calming. I don't necessarily believe everything she says. In fact, a big part of me doesn't think that I should. But I do. And I realize while she's talking that there's such a big part of me that so badly needs my mother to know me better than I know myself.

I let her convince me that I'm bipolar. I have Jackson request books from the library to read about it, and I decide to own it. It becomes who I am. It allows me to have faith in my mother and believe that I'm a generally good person who sadly has the odds stacked against her with this artists' disease.

I decide to track my mood changes throughout the day since it seems they flip around so often. I forget, though, that since I haven't been drinking, I've been smoking even more to make up the difference. When I look at my chart at the end of the week, month, and year, it's shocking that one can survive like that.

Anything can be what I'm learning is called a trigger.

And because I know that it's like a little plastic piece that comes along with my package of the bipolar illness, I justify it. I let myself believe that being triggered is beyond my control, which is like a license to stop trying.

Jackson starts questioning if my gripes with him are valid or just my illness rearing its head. He stops taking my thoughts and feelings seriously—as if he can't trust or respect them. Then I learn that he's been sharing extremely personal things about me with his friends as a means of support for himself. My privacy requirements take the backseat to his therapeutic needs, and I find this infuriating.

I want to leave Jackson, but every time I try, he cries, yells, and guilts me. He's unable to rationalize or be objective in these times. The first time it happened, he broke down in front of me, throwing himself across the room trying to regurgitate into the kitchen trash. His emotions are so volatile and foreign to me. They paralyze me into submission.

So instead, I leave him temporarily by smoking from the pipe and dragging the blade. I pretend to leave everyone who says they want to love me but end up making me suffer. It's not their fault. It's my fault. I'm the only constant here, so it's got to be me. After all, I'm the one who keeps letting them trigger me.

I write feverishly when I'm in a state like this. My creative juices never flow so rapidly as when I'm on the verge of taking my own life. There's something about the now or never, the rev of it all, that spins me for miles and miles.

Sometimes I go out into the street alone in the middle of the night. I walk around looking at the city in the dark, wondering about all the people sleeping so vulnerably close to one another. There are times when I spot another person wandering around on his own too. Part of me wants him to come and get me—take me away from my troubles. But part of me is still scared to die, so I scurry back home and lock the door, peering out to see how long the stranger lurks outside.

Barely scraping by on scattered freelance design gigs, I don't have health insurance. I find an ad, though, that promises free treatment and medication to people like me. So I schedule an interview to see what they can do for me and what I need to do in return.

I show up prepared with my mood charts and stories of insomnia, intense dreams and nightmares, volatile friendships and relationships, and everything else they eat up. Within a half-hour, the doctor quickly diagnoses me as a rapid cycling bipolar and assures that they can help. All I need to do is report to them how my medicine feels.

I tell the doc that I've read about certain medications not being effective if you take them and stop, the side effects they can have, and how they have ruined some lives.

"What happens when the study is over," I ask, "and I can't afford to keep up with the meds?"

The doctor shrugs. "You'll have to file for free insurance," he says.

"I've been trying to for six months already," I tell him. "The process sucks."

"Why don't you just try it out and see if what we prescribe helps? That's what you need to be focusing on right now—just finding something that helps you," he says.

In some twisted sense, I'm relieved to be given a diagnosis. There are so many things I don't know about myself that just having someone put a label on me is major.

I'm declared mentally ill. Yay?

A couple of books list Kurt Cobain as having been bipolar. In my distorted view, it makes me feel special and connected to Kurt. I decide it's no wonder I relate to so much of his music. I add that to my virtual identity card and almost wish there were a badge that came with it.

Rather than just giving in and joining the bipolar med testing program, I do a little more research and discover homeopathy. I find a local homeopath and schedule a meeting with her as soon as possible, figuring I can always try more extreme measures if this doesn't work.

There's a calmness and air about her that I connect to right away. She listens to everything I have to say in a manner in which no one has ever done with me. It's without judgment, without finger pointing in any direction, and with a sympathetic levelness. She spends three hours asking questions but mostly just letting me get out everything I have to share.

A few weeks later, I receive an envelope with a remedy inside another envelope. I look doubtfully onto it as I prepare it as instructed. How one tiny sugar pellet can be powerful enough to break through all of my issues leaves me skeptical at best. Yet, at the same time, there was something about her that led me to open my mind and try it. I also vow to stay off the weed for a bit to give the remedy a better chance.

I had read about how finding the right remedy could take much patience and time. That, coupled with my skeptical nature, has me surprised when I wake feeling different one day—maybe a week later.

After Pilates, sitting on the floor of my bedroom, facing the window, a cloud moves in the sky which allows the sun to splash onto me. I breathe in slowly, feeling somewhat familiar with another time—like a déjà vu—yet I can't quite place it. I head down to make myself breakfast, and the sky moves and splashes the sunbeam onto me once again. I sit there eating strawberries and toast, wondering how I feel so good inside.

I report back to the homeopath, who isn't as surprised as I am. She's delighted. I tell her that my intellectual side wants to call this coincidental, and she explains that it's a common effect. I wonder if just abstaining from the alcohol and weed could be the reason for my change. She agrees that it could be part of it but asks me if I crave drinking or smoking weed. And somehow, despite how much I've polluted my body for years, I don't.

MAX & LACEY

Feeling fueled by my revised state of being, I decide it's time to seek out a band. I've got so many songs now and am getting better at singing and playing without staring at my hands. I post links to my bedroom recordings on Craigslist.

The bulk of the people responding to me have links to music that makes me cringe. Some of the others are worth meeting, but one of them really excites me. It's a guy who plays with a girl he used to be in a signed band with. They have their own home studio, tons of gear, and links to music that I think is awesome. It's almost too good to be true.

Max picks me up one sunny afternoon. He steps out of the car with his rock 'n' roll hair, velvet pants, and a seventies coat. He has bright blue eyes and a seasoned ease about him. He throws my guitar in the back, and I ride with him to the house he just bought with his unbelievably attractive girlfriend, Lacey. We all hit it off amazingly well.

We head downstairs to play. Their setup is nothing I

could have imagined. There are walls of amps and cabs to choose from. Everything is miked and fed up through the wires in the walls to the mixing studio upstairs.

I'm nervous at first, as I've never really sang and played like this in front of many people—let alone these beautiful pros. But once I get started, I relax a little. And once I stop worrying about my own playing, I begin to notice that the tempo is hard to keep because the drums are speeding up and slowing down.

Max starts hitting a joint to level off. He says his medication is making him a little too rushed. Lacey seems to be cool with it, so I tell myself this is just how it's done in rock 'n' roll.

We play a few more songs, and things are okay minus the tempo situation. Max says we should get together in a couple days and try again when he's not having these problems.

Listening to the rough recording upstairs, he begins, "Have you ever," and then cuts himself off to say, "Well, of course you've dreamed of making an album, right?"

"Not in a very long while," I say, smiling.

"You've got a lot of great songs," he says. "We've totally gotta make an album together. We can do it for free right here."

I'm not used to anyone being so excited about my music. Although today didn't sound very good, I've never been in a band before, so I don't know how hard it is for everyone to play along together. Besides, these people were good enough to be signed to a label.

I start to absolutely adore Lacey. Despite being five years older than me, she's youthful, fun, and so excited about music. She's incredibly talented, and I can't understand why they want to work on my music at all. They seem to have plenty of her songs to work with. She tells me they just needed some neutral ground.

Jackson's happy to hear how well things went but gets jealous when I tell him how hot they are.

"We're hotter," he says, without even having seen them first.

"It's not a contest," I say with a smirk.

"Yeah it is," he says, grinning but serious.

MOTHER(LESS)LAND

When Jackson runs through his savings, he begrudgingly goes back to working for the man. As a gainfully employed microelectronic engineer, he gets issued a work trip that will take him to Seoul for one month.

"You're going to where I was born?" I say in disbelief.

"You can come if you want," he says. "I'll be working most of the time though."

"I don't know if I can afford it," I say.

"All you really need is airfare," he says.

I never really imagined I'd want to go to Korea at this point in my life, but there's something very wrong-feeling about my white boyfriend going there without me. The more I think about it, the crazier not going sounds.

I ask my next-older sister to borrow plane fare. Knowing what a big trip it is for me, she doesn't hesitate to help. I book my ticket a couple of days later, and we leave in a couple of weeks.

I spend some time painting with oils on canvas as a way to process what I'm going through. I begin to have dreams—strange seasick dreams—of being dropped off by my birth mother. In one dream I even see her face and, despite it being my own imagination, am still shocked to see someone who looks so much like me.

I have another dream that when I'm born, I start crying but am not supposed to be heard. My mother covers my mouth, so my chest pumps up and down but no sound is allowed to squeak through. I wonder to myself if that's why I hate crying.

My nightmares start coming back—dreams of fighting off intruders, rescuing the ones I love from crumbling floorboards, and shooting with guns that don't fire. I see blood, so much blood, in my dreams. It frightens me to know my mind is still capable of creating this level of horror. But nothing really makes them stop.

Oftentimes in my dreams I'm not even myself. I can be a tall skinny black man with a son. I can be a blonde white woman or a German soldier. I've been children in pre-civilization. Or I'm a superhero when I dream lucidly and am able to take control of the situation.

Jackson gets a Rosetta Stone DVD set from the library to learn Korean. The only problem is, it's disk thirteen to twenty-four, which doesn't work the way immersion is supposed to. I find a phrase book and a *Lonely Planet* but am nowhere near prepared for the trip. Language is just a small piece of it. My homeopath gives me a few different envelopes of remedies—just in case—and says to email her if I think I need help.

It takes us twenty-eight hours to get from Boston to

Chicago to Seattle to Tokyo to Seoul since I'm on a tight budget. I'm too emotionally drained from the turbulence and physically cramped from the travel to be anything but a witness to the most foreign place I've ever been. Somehow I expected familiarity to seep in and push some buttons that were waiting to be pushed.

The first couple of days are the hardest. While Jackson's studiously working day and night, I'm finding it hard to get on. No one seems to understand my English or my concerted efforts to speak the little I've learned from the phrasebook. Even trying to get lunch wears me out—never mind my supermarket fail to find detergent for washing laundry.

It's January of 2006, and I'm struck by how rich of a city Seoul is. There are skyscrapers, fancy cars, and kids running around with mobile phones like I've never seen. Everyone is dressed pretty much the same with clean lines and simple patterns. Makeup is applied to look as if there isn't any, and I can't help but notice the prevalence of plastic surgery. Every subway car has at least one ad on display, and many people don't even bother concealing the scars, the swelling on their noses, or new double-lids.

My eyes have always been difficult for me to accept. The flat, single lid that makes fashionable makeup nearly impossible has pissed me off more often than not. The reflection of my cheeks and monolids makes me ill, but I expected to fit in here. Not the case. With my hot pink-streaked hair, black eyeliner, and bright lipstick, I do not blend in here in the least.

When I'm able to get someone to help me find my way to wherever I'm headed, I'm usually asked if I'm Japanese.

No one wants to believe I'm one of them. And while I'm sure I confuse them with my lack of Korean language skills, it hurts to feel shunned from my supposed people. I can't help but feel rejected again from the one place in which I was supposed to belong.

Jackson has been having quite the opposite experience, being a white American man. People are only too happy to talk to him, to learn about him, and to help with directions and translations. I try to tell him that being here is rough for me but with his work responsibilities, he doesn't have any emotional bandwidth to offer. Instead, he marvels at how he sees my features in the rest of the Korean women around us. We get into an argument because he can't understand how I feel objectified and reduced by his observations. His perspective and the Korean people's perspectives of me make me dizzy. I can't remember when I've felt more alone.

Perhaps out of stubbornness, I make the decision to try to enjoy being in my birth country despite the language barrier and the odds between myself, my boyfriend, and the Koreans. At night I research places to visit and how I'll get there. This is not very easy because most of the stations' signs are only written in Hangul. To make matters worse, the country is in the midst of changing their romanization. For instance, in my most recent phrasebook they use Ch's and T's while the signage uses J's and D's. I don't want to have to decode everything on the fly, so night-before planning is crucial.

On my own, I join an English-speaking guided tour to visit a palace, Insadong's shopping street, and the amethyst mines. I wander in awe through sculpture park after gallery after museum and sprawling markets packed with people and tentacles. I see legless men on their bellies on skateboards with cassette players strapped to their backs with a basket for donations. It's cold, freezing cold, and all the young girls are in the tiniest miniskirts. I don't know how they manage.

Something about being here sparks the idea that I should visit the adoption agency I'm from. As far as I know, I was there for six months. After nearly a week of effort, I manage to get someone to speak English to me and schedule an appointment.

The morning of, I wake from a brutal nightmare in which I was murdered in the bathroom. Someone in my dream had broken in and slashed me over and over. I'm thankful for the alarm that puts it to an end.

Finding Holt is somewhat difficult, and when I arrive, I'm drawn a map to another building five minutes away. The sign on the door says *Post-Adoption Services*. It makes me realize that I'm just one of many other adoptees coming here hoping to find something connecting them to their beginnings.

When I get up to the room, I have difficulty finding the woman I spoke with over the phone. There's no reception desk, no door to knock on, and no bell to ring. Instead, there are about eight or ten older Korean women in an open room who ignore me. Some of whom decide to glance at me, cover their mouths, and snicker. I'm at a loss, so I stand there awkwardly hoping for someone to come to my rescue.

A stern-looking woman approaches minutes, which feel like days, later. She motions for me to back out and enter a shabby little conference room. She has a manila folder in her hands, which I'm fixated on. She motions for me to sit across from her at the laminated conference table.

"Have you ever seen your file before?" she asks, barely looking up to greet my eyes.

"No," I say, shaking my head.

"Not even the one your parents have?" she asks.

I say, "No," again, not sure that my parents have one.

In this dimly lit, outdated room, this unpleasant stranger proceeds to tell me things that contradict what I thought I've known my whole life.

"You were found in Daegu outside the hospital on March 19," she says. "You were admitted to the White Lily Orphanage in Daegu in which they estimated your birthday to have been on March 5. You were submitted to Holt on March 27, stayed at the White Lily for two months, and were with a foster mother for four."

The woman, Young, looks up to what must be my shocked expression and says, "Is this what you were told?"

"No," I say, confused. "Are you sure that's my file?"

She reads off my parents' names and our old address. "Is that right?"

I nod my head. "But I was told that I was left at the doorstep of a police station in Seoul," I tell her, "when I was just a day old. I never heard of Daegu or the orphanage."

My entire history is rewritten, yet Young appears unaffected. "I can give you the telephone number to the orphanage if you'd like," she says. I nod, submissively, feeling stripped of all power.

Young passes me off to someone friendlier who takes me on a short tour of the agency. We walk through hallways that are decorated with photos of Korean babies with their new white families, taped onto brick walls. In another hall, she points out a special wall displaying babies who were adopted to celebrities. Their photos are mounted on colorful construction paper that's cut into cute little frames.

I visit a room full of babies in limbo waiting for the final go-ahead to be shipped all over the world and given a new everything. Again, the Korean Orphan Protection Program springs to mind, but this time I can't laugh.

There's one baby girl who keeps crying in her crib, but none of the women tend to her. I peek in at her and notice she looks different from the others. I wonder if she is half white.

I've never had a maternal instinct toward human babies, but in this moment, I want to grab that crying little infant and run. I want to squeeze her and tell her that life's going to be okay. And then I stop myself in the tracks of my own romanticized fantasies and swallow the harsh truth.

I don't know that it will be—for her, for the others, and not even for me.

THE ORPHANAGE

My visit to the adoption agency is so grueling that I don't want to do anything heavy the next day. I don't want to take in the culture, go shopping, or even think about the orphanage. Instead, I come up with the brilliant plan to visit the Seoul Grand Park Zoo.

Stepping off the train, I'm immediately struck by the beauty back-splashed with the mountains. Korea is seventy percent mountain, I learn. The zoo grounds are absolutely breathtaking. There are endless animals to look in on, but I feel as though for every exhibit I approach, I'm crashing another happy couple's magic moment. And the closer I look, the animals don't look very happy.

I start to draw parallels between the caged animals to the cribbed babies at the adoption agency on my post-adoption tour. It tugs at a nerve knowing that these beautiful creatures were likely taken from their natural habitats in order to benefit others—myself included.

I try to put everything miserable out of my head and just enjoy what I can. One carefree day of mindlessness is all I need, yet so hard to come by.

The next day I make calls to the orphanage until someone who speaks English finally picks up. I make an appointment for early the next week and book my three-hour trip on the bullet train.

Straight away, Daegu seems to be a much poorer city than the cosmopolitan Seoul. I'm turned down by a few taxi drivers but luckily one accepts my poorly scribbled Korean on a piece of paper that says where I'm to go. It's not easy to find either. We jam in and back out of streets and alleys like a seasick amusement park ride.

The White Lily is no longer an orphanage. It's been converted to a daycare center and also serves as a convent. Many of the same nuns who cared for us abandoned babies are still there in a slightly different capacity. There have been extensive renovations, but the English-speaking sister is able to point out a few rooms I must've stayed in.

I play with the kids for twenty minutes or so, and a few of them follow us around on my tour, bowing and saying hello. There's something nice about knowing all these kids have homes to go to and aren't waiting to be sent somewhere new.

Unfortunately, the White Lily doesn't have any paperwork for me. They say there was a fire and many of our files were destroyed. They instead offer me a couple of cute ceramic plates and coffee. I don't drink coffee but sip it out of respect. We sit at the table awkwardly until I decide it's time to go.

The English-speaking sister takes me to see the kids

playing outside while we wait for my cab to arrive. Watching the children running, carefree, around her softens me. Although I've never wanted to have kids, I'd toyed with the idea of adopting a Korean baby someday. I tell the sister this.

"I feel like I'd understand in a way no one else would," I explain.

The sister smiles and without hesitation says, "That's nice, but I want you to have your *own* baby. That's better." She pats her stomach to make sure I understand.

I harden up, swallowing her words, and force a smile and a nod.

When the cab arrives, I thank her for her time and hospitality, and she wishes me well. She tells the driver that I want to go to Dongsan Hospital, and we wave goodbye, separated by the dirty window.

There's another outdoor market across from the hospital, so I take some time to look around as a buffer between two intense visits. The people of Daegu seem a little more raw than the Koreans in Seoul with their clothing, double lids, and posture. They still make a point to show their distaste for me, but I shake it off this time. I have bigger things crushing down on me.

Strangely enough, there's something familiar about the men here. I can't place it, but it sticks with me as I wander about. And then it hits me: The men of Daegu remind me of my father—not my Korean birth father but my Italian American adoptive father. They're all around his height and weight with salt and pepper side-parted hair, wearing sweaters with banded waists. It's uncanny.

Eventually I realize I can't postpone getting to the hospital much longer. I have a scheduled ticket back to Seoul in a couple of hours. I make my way over to the brick buildings and walk solemnly through the grounds.

The weather in South Korea much resembles the New England weather that I grew up in. The winters have a bite in the air. The anniversary of when I was found here is in seven weeks. I wonder who would leave a baby outside in the cold winter weather.

My eyes scan from tree to rock to bush, and I wonder how much the landscaping has changed over time. I wonder where exactly I might have been left, and how long I was out in the winter weather before being found.

I want to think about the woman who carried me in her womb and gave birth to me. I want to consider the circumstances that were so awful to make such a big decision for the both of us. I want to wonder how hard it was for her and whether or not she carried on with her day with no one the wiser. I want to feel empathetic for this woman, my physical mother, but I can't. Instead, I revert to a child and can't stop sympathizing with the possibly two-week-old me.

What if no one had found me in time, and I froze to a crisp? How scary must it have been to be dropped off by the one person I depended on and for her to never return?

It's no wonder anymore why I've always had to be the one leaving everyone first—so they couldn't leave me. All those times I packed my room, hoping to run away but with nowhere to go... And then, I stayed with people who didn't treat me well because it felt safer than being alone.

It makes sense now why I wasn't able to make the right decision to let Jasminn go without waking her up from the surgery that day. I didn't want to be as bad as I perceived my birth mother to be, leaving me to die on my own.

And the panic that set in when Seamus kept disappearing was probably such a trigger because of all this.

My whole life, I've been desperately fearful of being left. The hint of abandonment reopened a primal wound and left me helpless—the way I must've felt that day, waiting to be discovered and brought in to shelter by the one who was supposed to love me.

There's a maddening thought materializing. It's not born from the moment so much as awakened by it. In a fuzzy, transparent image I see myself step out of my body and over to an unmarked spot on the grass. This vision of me slits her wrists and falls to the ground. It's almost poetic, despite the horror.

I turn around and leave her there.

BEING FOUND

When we return home from Korea, things with Jackson never really improve. My homeopath says that my remedy picture has changed, which is supposed to be a good thing. I'm on a new remedy now, and I'm not sure if it's to be credited, but I'm finding working through my breakup less emotional than I would have in the past. I feel brave enough to push through Jackson's sadness and guilt, knowing that if I don't think he's the one for me then he'll be better off in the long run too.

My birthday is exceptionally shitty this year, however. It's the first time I know for sure that it isn't my actual birthday. There's a deep-seated sadness that's difficult to shake. I just feel more alone than before, somehow, despite feeling confident in pursuing my breakup. It's an odd cocktail of emotions.

I tell my friends and family that I don't think I want to celebrate my birthday on record anymore. Perhaps, I suggest, I should celebrate the day I was found, which is three days later. Nobody challenges me on this, thankfully. But it's not like they were going to really celebrate with me in person anyway.

I spend my first known Found Day making music. Working on a new song feels like the perfect gift to myself. I lose myself in it for several hours and record a rough demo.

In late afternoon I take a break and check my email. There's a new message from an unknown address. I nearly send it to spam but decide to open it when I see the title says, "Korean Adoptee." It reads:

This may seem a little unusual. I am also a Korean Adoptee. I am now thirty-four years old and throughout my thirty years in the United States, I have had sporadic urges to research more about Korea. I haven't returned to Korea since my adoption but have always dreamed of returning one day. I stumbled across your website today when I Googled the White Lily Orphanage. I was completely blown away by your journal and pictures. I can't explain what a gift you have given to me on this sunny, cold Michigan day. I have enjoyed my Korean journey vicariously through yours, and your pictures and entries had me mesmerized for hours. It is so nice to know that there are other people in this world with a similar story. It makes me not feel so alone.

I'm not sure I can truly express how much you have given to me today. You are so much better with words. You have given me so much by seeing the orphanage and giving me some insight of where I am from. I will never be able to thank you enough, from the bottom of my heart, thank you!

I sit there, rereading the email a few times with my jaw

dropped. Chills shoot across my skin. I'm in awe of this letter. And what's even more incredible is the day it arrives: On my first known Found Day, I'm found once again by a fellow adoptee that passed through the same orphanage.

When I'm able to gather myself from the emotional impact, I send a response. We share several emails and stories about our lives, our many failed relationships, and so much more.

Two weeks later I get a similar email. This happens again and again. Within months there's almost a dozen of us. So one of the girls encourages me to create some sort of online group. I agree that we need a place where we can all connect. I start a forum where even more people from all over the world begin to find us.

It starts off light. I create fun surveys that help us get to know one another. So many of us seem to have been adopted into white families in areas where there weren't many other Asians. Some have other Korean adoptee siblings. Some have one or two other white siblings who were born biologically from their adoptive parents. A couple had tracked down their birth families, and that opens up so many difficult feelings and questions for the rest of us to consider.

I've always been so angry at my Koreanness. I felt like my face was telling a lie and hated the way it separated me from the rest. I was insecure from being from a place people rarely heard of, and from the way they poked fun at an assumed and outdated version of its culture. I felt intimidated by the *true Koreans* who were raised there—or here in unbroken families.

Oddly enough, the biggest thing that made me an outlier

up till now is the thing that unifies me to a population I didn't know existed. We call ourselves The Lilies, named after the White Lily Orphanage. Over time, our bonds with one another begin to fill a void that most of us hadn't been able to articulate before.

Not only do I begin to feel less alone in the world, but I begin to feel special. Being found again by my extended family—some of whom were at the orphanage when I was—gives me something to feel thankful for. Had I not been adopted and gone through what I have, I'd have no connection to any of these beautiful people.

At last, we're connected to a piece of ourselves that no one else in our adoptive lives understands. There's a built-in compassion and license to express things we may have been too ashamed or afraid to feel and share until now.

Many tears are shed together. And through this thera-peutic outlet, I begin to connect the real dots. Others begin to connect their dots too. Together, we begin to heal our-selves from the residual emotions pent up for decades.

REPOSESSION

Although friendship with my new bandmates, Max and Lacey, is deepening, the music is dwindling. We record a couple of tracks, but Max's substance abuse is becoming too
desperate for him to focus on music for long enough spans
of time. It's a terrible thing to witness, as I can see its
power over him. He has so much talent. Both he and Lacey
should be superstars by now, but they're battling so much
between them and within themselves to do much else.

I've started playing with my ex-roommate, Val, and her
ex-roommate, Terri. We're pretty punk rock. It's not as pro-
sounding as the recordings I made with Max and Lacey, but
we have fun every time we're together. The mood is light
and easy, and there are always many laughs. And I so need
the sweet release of laughter these days.

Val, the bassist, is a cute lesbian who's been playing in
bands since high school. Same with Terri—minus the lesbian part. She's got tattoos all over her body. All of Val's

lesbian friends and all my straight guy friends are crazy about her. It's really fun to witness the wave of awe when she walks in the room.

I haven't been playing guitar for very long and am limited instrumentally. I work with what I have to write songs and am still kind of shocked that anyone good is willing to play with me in a band.

Aside from all the fun that we have laughing and drinking beer, it's a magical time in my life. I'm making music with people. I don't have delusions of rock stardom, but it's a piece of me that I thought I'd resigned forever after *The Incident* half a lifetime ago.

Val has been anxious to get back up on stage, as it's been over a year since she and her ex-bandmate played live. "We need to make demos and send them to clubs," she says. "I think we're ready."

"How are we going to do that?" I ask, concerned about the drums.

"We just need to set up some mics and feed them into the PA," says Val.

"Ooh—maybe we can plug the PA directly into your computer," says Terri.

And so we run with our excitement, test-miking and recording until we get something that sounds imperfectly punk rock. We upload a few songs to our MySpace page and start sending out emails to clubs. In almost no time at all, we have three shows booked.

Back in the days of my solo shows, things were very different. There was no one else to look at, no one else to listen to, and most importantly, no one else to share any of it with.

"I think I know what I'm going to wear," I say, grimacing at practice. "A black skirt, a black and white shirt, frilly knee socks, and black and white bows in my hair."

"What color bows are you going to wear in your hair, Val," jokes Terri, as Val is not quite femme.

"I'm thinking pink," she says, throwing back a Miller Lite.

In Val's basement where we practice, we've installed a disco ball on the ceiling. Terri's drums are in the front corner—the first thing you see as you walk down the stairs from the kitchen. The walls are old school wood panels, but we dressed them up with fabric from a Dollar Store run. Just like the recordings, everything is imperfectly perfect. We have our little rock den.

Terri's a photographer and says we need band photos to use for our posters. The clubs require us to make and distribute posters and fliers in and out of the clubs. So we go on a field trip to Castle Island in South Boston with Terri's boyfriend who agrees to man the camera. We walk around searching for good photo ops and pose when the locations feel right. It's hilarious, really, like everything else we do, because we have three distinctively different personalities and styles that make it so.

When the link to the photos gets passed around, though, another demon of mine is awakened. I'd forgotten how uncomfortable I am with the camera when someone else is behind the lens.

I've been working on finding acceptance in my appearance on my own since digital cameras came in. I'm brave enough to explore creative concepts in which I'm the subject in my photos, I suppose. I even share some on my

LiveJournal and MySpace pages. But it's been a long time since I've seen myself as I am, photographed by somebody else. I really struggle with it.

"I don't know if I like the way I look in these," I say, cringing, to the girls.

"What, are you kidding?" says Terri. "You look cool! What's wrong with these pictures of you?"

But it's hard to explain how I'm still not used to seeing the real shape of my face, my crooked smile when I laugh, or the side-profile that highlights my Asianness. Even though I can now appreciate other people's Asian looks and feel good about my new Lily family, it's awfully complex. I still don't look like how I feel on the inside.

I talk privately with Val about the photos, and she convinces me that they're cool and we should go with them. She also shares that she thinks Terri might have a crush on her since there are so many photos of Val alone. We giggle together, wondering if Terri might be bisexual. I giggle to myself over the confidence Val has. It's a refreshing attitude that I'm not used to and I love it.

It's been so long since I had girl friends like this. Roz moved to Colorado with her husband and so it's been a while since I had any girl time. I bring Lacey—the first bassist I was working with—into our group and we all go on bowling, beer, and beach excursions. It's like my second chance at being young, healthy, and free. For so long, I'd chosen to stay isolated in unhealthy relationships, afraid to drag anyone else into my world of doom.

Life begins to feel balanced. I'm renewed with a better understanding of who I am and who I want to be. So I push to finalize the ending with Jackson. It's not easy. We're both caring for his cat that is sick, but I know there will always be an excuse and that it's time to move on. We try to stay friends, and it's tough at first, as he has such a hard time letting go. But I don't take it personally, as I know that he's always had difficulty moving on from past loves.

As our first show quickly approaches, Val gets the idea to have a pre-show basement show. We have plans to hit the roller derby on Cinco de Mayo, and she decides that the perfect time for the party is right after the derby. Needless to say, I barely take in the roller derby at all as I freak out to myself in my head.

These fears feel justified and probably common, but there's an underlying fear that I can't quite place. It's like an itch that you just can't seem to hone in on, so you keep scratching everywhere, hoping to find it by mistake.

APRIL 1991 //
IN THE SPOTLIGHT

I'm standing on the side of the stage, waiting to be announced. It's another talent showcase, and I've prepared something special for this particular show. This club is a legit dance club for adults, and the last time I sang here I totally bombed. I was nervous because a bunch of boys were here to see me. They were looking for an act to dance with and were checking me out. It was the absolute worst, and I felt like such shit about it for months. I'm determined to make up for it now.

My oldest sister drove me here and is standing in the back with a promoter who's always shown interest in me. He shows a different kind of interest in my sister, who's much closer to his age. I spot them as she waves over to me, and I groan inwardly, not wanting to feel like a child. I mean—I just turned sixteen.

I'm in black pants, a bejeweled bustier, and a black hat

that makes my well-lined eyes stand out. I try to psyche myself up.

You're gonna kill it. Come on, you need to show everyone that you can do it. There's no way you can mess this up again. Let's go!

They announce my name, and the crowd begins to cheer as the dance mix I dubbed starts to play through the speakers. I emerge onto the stage in full-force, hitting every move I choreographed to a T. The lights above me go wild, splashing colors around the room. There are some crowd pleaser samples that are popular within the black community. I put them in there strategically and they work, as the crowd stage right are jumping from their seats to salute me. And then my mix fades out, and the music I made with my Korg M1 fades in. It slows down, and I catch my breath. I start singing along—which is harder than I expected, given the amount of energy I put into my dance. But I push through with my mid-tempo LL Cool J-style rap and melodic chorus. It seems to go by so fast, and the audience is standing, cheering voraciously.

After my show, I'm buzzing so high and feeling so proud of myself. I really did it. Not only did I make up for last time, but I got a reaction much greater than I ever expected. People are coming up to talk to me.

"Yo, that shit was dope!"

"I couldn't believe you sampled that bit in there!"

And, "Girl, you sing and dance like a sistah." *Snap! Snap! Snap!*

My sister and the promoter have a look of awe across their faces. They look at me as if they don't even know me.

"Wow! Good job, Millie," says my sister.

"I didn't know you had it in you!" says the promoter.

The rest of the night is a blur until I find myself at home in bed. I go over the show in my head, trying to picture it from the outside. I see the faces of the crowd as I'm doing my thing and later on, when I'm coming off the stage. Mostly, it's the look of approval and acceptance from the other minorities—the Blacks and the Latinos—that really leaves me feeling satisfied. I've always felt subpar to them and their skills, secretly wishing I were more like them. I wonder what it might have been like to be raised among other cultures instead of the white world that I know.

MAY 4, 1991 //
THE INCIDENT

I can't believe he would do this to me. I thought Roger was my friend. He said he just had to change his clothes—yet I waited and waited for him to come out. I find him sitting in his room watching TV, so I say, impatiently, "Are you ready yet? Come on. We've gotta get to the party."

Roger says, "Nah, man. I just figured we'd hang."

Fuming, I say, "And you were going to tell me this when?" I look at him, glaring, as he eats fries and keeps watching TV.

"Take me home then," I say, infuriated.

"I can't," he says, barely taking his eyes off the TV for a moment to look at me.

"Why not?" I demand more than ask.

"My brother took the car. He won't be back for hours."

I dart out of his room and over to the window that overlooks the driveway. Sure enough, the red car we arrived in is gone.

I can't really think straight as my head fills with rage. I try to breathe. I open up the sliding glass door to the balcony and see this other guy I know heading in.

"Ace, can you give me a ride to a party?" I ask as he enters the room.

Ace is a rather large man—probably nearing about three hundred pounds. He towers over me with his broad, thick shoulders, looks down at me and says, "If you give me a blow job."

Disgusted, I huff loudly and head out to the balcony, trying to collect my thoughts. I've always known Ace was a sketchy guy, but Roger was supposed to be my friend. I can't get over how badly he deceived me.

As I sulk to myself, a group of guys are approaching from down the road. They see me and call up.

"Hey, that's that girl," says one of them excitedly.

"Do I know you? You look familiar," I say as they near.

"We were at the club a couple weekends ago," says one. "Saw your act. That shit was the shit!"

Unable to help being flattered, I say, "Thanks! I had a lot of fun."

"Whatchu doin' out here?" he asks, darting his eyes to the guys in the apartment.

And so I decide to share my woes. "These guys aren't my friends. I thought that they were, but they've proven to be nothing but lying assholes."

"Damn," says another, chuckling.

"One of them was supposed to take me to a party. And then I get here and all of a sudden his car goes missing. Then he says that he never intended to take me to the party in the first place! So now I'm stranded down here," I huff, shaking my head.

One of them shakes his head with me. "Man, that's fucked up," he says. "Don't they realize that you're a person too? Come with me. I'll give you a ride."

I look back into the apartment and see Roger and Ace laughing. "Don't go with him," they say. "He don't even have a car!"

I glare at them with narrowed eyes and say, "And I'm supposed to trust you?"

I get my coat and storm out of the apartment, meeting the boys on the street. We walk toward tough-looking kids swinging baseball bats in their hands. They say, "Yo," and we carry on passing all kinds of badass-looking people. At first, I can't get over how friendly they are to us despite their appearances. And then I realize that I must be with a well-respected crew.

As we continue our walk to Al's house, our crew starts to taper off. Approaching his place, I see an elderly woman on the third floor. She's got a white Afghan blanket wrapped around her shoulders as she peers down into the street.

"Where's your car?" I ask, heading up the front steps.

"I gotta call my boy to come bring it," Al says. "He's just across the way."

But once inside the front door, things begin to feel different. I've never seen a place like this before, and it's a lot to take in.

The door opens up into a narrow hallway. The white walls are banged up and dingy and have nothing hanging from them. It leads us around a slight bend to a doorless opening. There's a kid about my age standing there in the kitchen, wearing a colorful propeller cap with *Trivial Pursuit*-like wedges. They're kind of a thing I've been noticing some city kids wearing. He looks at us but doesn't speak.

I say, "Hi," out of habit, really, because it's rude not to acknowledge someone's presence when you're in his house. He just sort of nods at me a little, disengaged.

The hallway bends back toward the front, and Al nudges me along past one closed door toward another. He opens it up and again, I'm caught off-guard by the state of the place. There's nothing but a couple of unkempt mattresses on the floor with a little space heater between them.

I hear the door close behind me. I know something feels wrong but am perhaps falsely secured by the thought of the boy in the kitchen and the old woman on the third floor. I look over to the two windows that are covered with make-shift curtains and then over to the right at Al shifting through his open closet. He pulls out a black gun and cocks it.

"Want one?" he says and throws a silver gun at my feet.

I pick it up, not knowing what else to do, as I'm completely out of my element. I'm not sure what comes over me, but I take it and say, "Like this?" as I motion to tuck it into my jacket.

"You down," he says, nodding at me with a smile.

And then he pulls out some baggies of powder. I assume it's cocaine or some other hard drug. He's throwing some baggies into a duffle bag on the floor as I stand there dumbfounded. I carefully place the silver gun on the floor.

In a flash, I'm lying back on the mattress with a gun pressed into my left temple. I'm squeezing my legs together as tightly as I can as he pries them open with one hand. He manages to remove my black leggings. My black dress is pushed up around my waist. It's all happening so fast that I don't really register what's happening. I just keep fighting with my body, pressing my legs together as tightly as I can.

He doesn't speak. He tries to kiss me, and I turn my head as he pushes his face into mine. Just the weight of his body on mine feels like I might fall into the mattress as the springs push awkwardly into my back and legs.

Somehow I'm pulled up off the mattress and onto my knees as they ache from the dirty wood floor. My head spins. He has a condom on and is pushing my head down onto him.

Why is this happening? How is this happening? What should I do?

The silver gun isn't far out of reach, and I'm half-tempted to try to grab it. And then I wonder if it's even loaded because why would he give me a loaded gun?

It crosses my mind to bite down hard on his dick and just run. But I realize that there's nowhere to run to. I quickly remember all the thugs on the street who were so friendly toward him. I don't imagine they'd let me get very far.

Apparently I'm not doing a good enough job, as I keep gagging and coughing. So I'm thrown back onto the mattress as he tries harder to push my legs open. And when he enters, the pain sends stars to my eyes, blinding me from the dirty ceiling. I squeeze tight, really tight like I learned in gymnastics, flexing all of the muscles in my body. And then I disappear. Al begins to fade out of view.

There's a blue sky with white fluffy clouds and I'm in it. I'm floating aimlessly above the rest of the world. I look down and see people waving up to me as I spread my arms wide, focusing hard lest I fall.

I close my eyes and just feel the soft clouds hit my belly and smile from the light tickle. I open my eyes back up and see my neighborhood.

Ah, home. That brick house with the flat stone walkway. The green grass and the large rock I used to sit on as a kid. And that weird stone donkey and cart on the lower lawn.

I fly closer and notice there are people in the driveway. It's my family. They smile, waving up to me. I wave back, wondering what they're doing out there. How'd they know I'd be flying above?

And then something changes. The blue skies turn grey and the clouds toughen up like wool. A woman comes and takes my hand.

"It's time to go now," she says.

I fly with her through the thundering sky. I trust her, but she lets go of my hand and drops me back down through the ceiling and onto the dirty old mattress. I feel the springs dig into my back again and the burn of betrayal. And then I feel puddles of warm goo trickle onto my stomach.

All I can think is, *My mother is going to kill me. Or maybe he'll kill me now. That would be better. Then I don't have to do anything anymore. I can just die and let them hate me for sneaking out. They'll probably be secretly delighted not to have to worry about me anymore.*

Al is up making calls, getting beeps on his pager, and peering out onto the street. I pull my dress down to cover myself up, drying the goo with the inside of the dress. I put my clothes on and glance over at the silver gun as my heart sinks further into my stomach.

Al catches my eye and says, "I can find out where you live. Don't think that I can't. I've been to prison before, and I ain't goin' back." There's an intense look in his eye that has me believe it.

Before I know it, Al is pulling me back out through the U-shaped hallway and onto the street. He shoves me into the back of a car with three other black guys—one moves from the driver's seat to let Al take the wheel.

Al says, "This is Yum Yum. She's going to be working for me. But I need to try her out on all you."

I don't speak. My eyes stare at the back of the seat in front of me until even the pores of the leather blur out.

"She's not very experienced, so y'all gotta train her. Can't be havin' no disappointed customers," he jokes.

He pulls the car over on the side of the road near a park. We file out of the car, and I have no fight left in me.

"Yo," he says, nodding to one of the men. "You take Yum Yum in back. Wear a rubber."

Al and two others stand on the sidewalk as the other sits in the back of the car with his feet spread out on the curb. His pants are down, and he's rolling a condom over himself.

"You gonna do this or what?" he says, flicking my head with his hand, and so I do.

There are no thoughts left of self-preservation or pro-tection. I'm unable to process anything anymore. I begrudg-ingly give him a blank look and gag just as soon as my mouth tastes the rubber.

"Go deep!" he orders.

I don't do it because I fear for my life. I do it because I simply don't know what else to do. But I gag and I choke because I can't do it. I can't physically do it.

"Nah, this is worthless," he calls over to Al, backhanding the side of my head. "She's no good. She's only gettin' the tip."

Al shoves another over my way as this one pulls up his pants.

The second guy pulls down his pants and somehow catches my eye. He unrolls the condom down and looks at me to start. My eyes meet his, warily.

"You don't want to be doin' this, do ya?" he whispers.

I subtly shake my head.

He yells, "Y'all gotta move down the street a bit more. I can't do this with y'all right there so close."

The three of them go down the road a little further.

"You all right?" he asks. "He hurt you?"

"He raped me," I hear myself say. "I was a virgin," I add, unsure why.

The guy shakes his head. "How'd you get involved with him? Al's a bad motherfucker," he says. "I don't know if I can help you."

Al's voice bellows over, "So whatcha think? She gonna make me some dough?"

"Nah, man," he yells, fixing his pants. "Like he said— she's no good for this. You should find someone else. I know a few I'll send over."

Al heads back toward us with the other two. I stand up and nearly fall down before grabbing the side of the car.

"Maybe she just need some more practice," says Al, looking me up and down.

"Nah, man," says the good one. "You best off gettin' yourself someone who knows what they be doin'."

"Back in the car," huffs Al.

The car is moving really slowly through the streets, as Al gets out every so often to make a deal with someone. I feel like I could throw up if I had the energy. This night might never end.

Someone else is at the wheel, and Al's bossing him around to go this way and that. We pull behind a building into a secluded driveway and Al says, "I'm out." My heart lifts, as I can hardly believe it. He opens his door and says, "Just after I get myself another blow job."

I'm not sure what comes over me at this point. Maybe it's that I feel so low that nothing matters anymore. I'm not worried about my life or what he might do to me. I reach from somewhere down around the pit of my being and yell out a long and echoing, "NOOOOOOOOO!"

The atmosphere in the car is intense. I can see that everyone's afraid of what Al might do. He gets out of the car, pierces his eyes at me, slams the door really hard and says, "Then fuck ya!"

It feels like an eternity between then and when the car starts up. We're all afraid he's going to turn around and start shooting. But he doesn't. The car soon carries on through the streets just as slowly as before.

I don't feel empowered. I'm no longer enraged. And I don't feel any sense of safety yet.

"Can you drive me home?" I say, cautiously.

"Where you live," asks the driver.

"Suburbs on the North Shore," I say.

"You got gas money?" he says.

"I have nothing," I say.

"Nah, then," says the driver.

"Man, just take her home," says the good one.

"No gas," he replies. "I'll drop you off somewhere around here."

"I don't know where I am," I say, wearily.

"Where'd you run into Al then?" he asks.

"Outside of a friend's house. Well, he's not my friend. He's the one who got me into this by lying to me," I say, not that any of that matters anymore. It all feels so far back in another lifetime.

All the cars are out now, filling the streets with booming basslines. People drive really slowly in pimped out cars with tinted windows. Side windows are down so you can see who's inside. The men all exchange subtle nods as they pass one another. It's a culture I've never seen before. There are so many cars filled with tough-looking men. And then I recognize a couple of faces.

"Hey, that's Roger and Ace," I say, as our eyes lock with one another.

"Aw, shit," they say, faces alit, in hysterics. "There she be!"

"I'll get out here," I say, "and go with those guys."

"You sure now?" says the good one.

I nod. He nods back.

In the back of Roger's car, I feel some weird sense of familiarity. It's not quite safety, but it's a small step up.

In the kitchen of Roger's apartment, I get myself a glass of water and stand there shaking.

"So what happened?" They want to know, looking almost too giddy.

"He raped me," I say, fighting back tears. I need to look tough. I don't know why, but I do. "And then he made me give a couple of those guys in the car a blow job."

"Damn," says Roger, shaking his head. "And you was a virgin, too, weren't ya?"

I nod my head sullenly. "Can you take me home now?" I ask.

Roger looks at Ace, so I look at him too.

"Not without a blow job," he says, grinning widely.

And it feels like a punch to the face.

"After what she just said she been through?" Roger says, as bewildered as I am.

"She can do it to them, she can do it to me," says Ace.

"I'm not doing it!" I say, defiantly. I can feel the heat in my cheeks as I yell.

"I'm goin' home then," says Ace with a smirk.

Roger just shakes his head as Ace walks out the door.

Alone with Roger, I can tell that although he was the one who initially deceived me, he's shaken from what has happened. He nervously rummages through cabinets and takes out a big pan, filling it with soap and water. And to my utter surprise, he sits down in a chair and washes his feet.

"All I can say is, I take no blame for what happened," he says. "I told you not to go with him. You didn't listen. I'm sorry it happened to ya, but you should've listened."

"Roger, you're the one who put me in the situation!" I say, slightly raising my voice. "If you hadn't tricked me into coming down here, leaving me stranded, I'd never have gone out on the balcony, and he'd never have seen me."

"But I told you, do not go with him," he says, shaking his head. "You wouldn't listen."

"And why should I have listened to you?" I say in disbelief. "You were supposed to be my friend, and you lied to me."

"I take none of the blame," he says again, washing his feet.

"Can I use your phone?" I say, glaring at him and his odd reactions.

I flip through my little phone book and page this guy I met in a dance club one night. He had thought I was older and when he found out I wasn't, he gave me his card and said, "Page me if you ever find yourself in trouble. But be careful. There are a lot of guys out there who won't care how young you are."

He's a bit of an Italian gangster, but there's something about him that I can relate to. Maybe it's because my family's Italian and growing up, we were often around guys like him in the North End. He calls me back right away and says he'll come pick me up.

"Listen, are you in trouble?" he asks.

"Yeah," I say.

"Anything bad happen?" he asks.

"I was raped," I say quietly.

"Give me your address. My cousin and I will be down a-sap," he says.

When he arrives in his fancy sports car, he gets out and looks Roger up and down really hard.

"He the one who did it?" he asks, nodding slightly.

"No," I say.

"Are you sure, now?" he asks.

And I say, "No. He wasn't."

I get into the tiny sports car and squeeze in between him and his cousin. His cousin has a gun between his thighs with his finger on the trigger just in case anything goes down.

On the way home, I tell them both what had happened.

"I'm gonna come in and help you tell your father," he says.

"No," I say, "I'm not telling them what happened."

"Look, I know this is hard, but you have to. I'll come in with you, and we'll tell him together. It'll be okay," he says.

"I can't. I have to tell them a lie. At least for now. I just can't," I say.

Together, we concoct a story. I decide to say I went out to a club but got kicked out and couldn't get back in. I'll say that I couldn't get a hold of anybody until now. I was afraid to have my parents pick me up, I'll say, because I didn't want to get in too much trouble. I'll say that I thought I'd make it home before them, but it didn't work out.

My mother, father, oldest sister, my Italian hero, and I, sit in the living room while I tell the lie. My father keeps asking questions, and I continue to lie, incriminating no one but myself. I can tell my father's not sure whether he can trust my Italian hero or not, but he shakes his hand and thanks him for bringing me home.

Once he's gone, the real inquisition sets in and the yelling and accusations begin. I listen to them scold me and tell me how much I worried them for about half an hour as I shrink into the warmth of the couch. And when the yelling stops, I manage the energy to walk down the hall to my room.

Oh, that room that I'd hoped to run away from so many times before. How welcoming it is now.

I remove my clothes and roll them up into a ball. Without thinking, I shove them into a plastic shopping bag and then push the whole thing into the back of a bottom drawer to deal with later. I put on some clothes, too tired to wash my face or brush my teeth. I can't even think about trying to clean off the sticky goo on my belly, so I leave it. I just need to lie down and crawl under my covers. It's all I am able to do.

No dog or cat nudges its way into my room tonight. I lie in bed alone, hyper-aware of every sound in and out of the house. I just want to feel nothing, hear nothing, see nothing, know nothing. Eventually, I must've fallen asleep.

WHITE LACE IN MY FACE

There's a lot of commotion outside my bedroom door in the morning. People are fighting over the bathroom across the hall. My mother walks in with tired eyes, says, "Get up," and leaves the door open.

She's annoyed that I kept them up late last night. Of course she doesn't know what I've really been through. And now today, of all days, I need to put on one of my sister's dresses and go to my cousin's wedding.

I always hate looking at my face in the mirror when I try to fix it up with makeup, but today it's especially pathetic. When I come out of the shower, my skin is blotchy from scrubbing it so hard. I pile on layers of foundation and try to make the most of the sore vision before me.

Socializing with extended family is awkward enough for me on the best of days. I don't fit in; I don't know what to say and can't seem to ever remember anyone's name or how we're supposedly related.

"What's wrong with Millie?" I see one of my cousins ask.

My mom glances over at me and back to her. She says, "Oh, just being a sulky teenager." They laugh.

I sit by myself in one of the many rooms of this gorgeous castle up on the North Shore. Everyone looks so nice and normal. Everyone looks like they belong. There's white lace and delicate flowers everywhere. I just want to liquefy myself into a puddle on the ground and seep into the grout till I'm gone.

My mother's sister is in the other room singing operatically about how her child has grown. She's a somewhat famous church singer. Her big deal is that she was invited to sing for the Pope.

Everyone and everything is just perfect.

I dreamt of this day for myself. I never bought any of those lies and myths from Catholic school. But there was something that appealed to me about saving myself for my wedding. I wanted a transformative day where all would see me as pure, beautiful, white, and special while I stood before the man of my dreams. I really believed that if I held back from the pressures of sex, that I'd be rewarded with a future to make up for being the ugly duckling I've been my whole life. And now I realize this day will never come. That dream has been shattered into a million sharp little pieces, and I feel like I've swallowed them all.

* * *

Being back in school is just as much of a blur as the wedding. I'm completely tuned out. I walk around in a haze, barely acknowledging friends or what I'm supposed to be learning.

This one girl who's always had complex love/hate feelings for me approaches as I walk into the cafeteria for lunch. She knows Roger and that crew because I've brought her down to the city a few times. At one point she tried to sing with me but froze from intense stage fright. She never had a passion for making music like I did anyway. She just really wanted the attention and to be around city kids, I think.

She says, "I heard a rumor about you," with a devilish smirk.

I look at her but don't say a word.

"So how was it?" she asks, squaring her shoulders in front of me so that I have to stop and stand there with her.

"Just shut up, please," I say, looking away from her face.

"Don't you dare fucking tell me to shut up," she says, leaning over me. She's got the better part of a foot on me and uses it to intimidate.

"Look, I don't want to fight," I say to her. "Just leave me alone, okay?"

"I heard you liked it," she says as I'm walking away.

I turn around and put my entire sixty-two inches in her face. I look up at her chin and say, beneath my breath, "I was raped! I was held at gunpoint, and you have no fucking idea what that's like."

I step back and see her hard face start to soften.

"I'm sorry," she says quietly.

"You have no idea!" I snap.

"But Roger says," she begins.

I cut her off. "Roger is the one who got me into the

whole mess, so I don't give a shit what Roger says! Don't tell me because I don't want to know!"

I storm off, fuming, not bothering to eat. I'm not hungry anyway.

I haven't been working on music at all. I start writing in one of my little blank books. Sitting in the closet in my wall one day, I decide to write the truth about what happened on May 4.

I must sit there for hours reading it over and over. It's just the basic emotionless facts scribbled out over three and a half pages.

I flash back to that time when I was small and my mother found my suicide letter. Behind my eyes, I imagine tearing this whole thing up and flushing it down that same toilet. But I can't bring myself to. I know that no matter what I do, this is something I can't fake as if it never happened.

I open the door to my room and just sit on the little hydraulic stool that I use for my synthesizer. My next-older sister walks by, and I call her in.

"What's up?" she asks.

I hand her the book and say, "Will you read this?" I have the page opened up to the beginning.

I look away from her as she stands there and reads it to herself. She says, "Did this really happen? When?"

I nod my head and say, "That night I was gone. Before the wedding."

She says, "Can I share this?"

I shrug.

Both older sisters come back into my room. The oldest is now holding the book and reading it furiously. She says,

"Millie, this is illegal! He can't get away with this!"

I tell her, "I can't do anything, or he'll come and get us. He might kill us all."

"We need to show Mom and Dad," she says. "Can I do that?"

I shrug again and then nod a small "yes."

The five of us sit around the kitchen table. I'm not sure what my sister said to them, but both of my parents look prepared to hear something awful.

"Do you wanna tell us what happened?" says my dad.

I shake my head slowly. I look over to my sisters, and the one up from me says, "I'll read it."

So we all listen as she reads the blunt facts of what happened a week or so ago. My oldest sister is crying, and I stare down at the table and let my eyes follow the little lines of the wood grain.

"Is that what really happened?" says my dad. "Why didn't you tell us? Why'd you have to lie to us that night?"

I can't speak.

And then he says, full of anger, "Was it that bastard who brought you home?"

I shake my head quickly. "No!" I say. "He's the one who saved me."

"Who was it, then?" says my father, demanding to know the truth.

"I don't know who he was," I say. "Just some guy who saw me perform at one of the showcases."

"We have to find who it was and press charges," he says matter-of-factly.

"We can't," I say. "He said he'd been to jail before and that he'll find out where we live if I say anything. He's got guns and sells drugs."

I don't know how else to say, *Dad, he's more powerful than you. I don't trust that you can protect us. Not even with your surveillance cameras and alarms.*

"Why didn't you shower that night?" asks my mother, now raising her voice.

"I don't know," I say. "I was tired."

"So you slept... *like that*?" she says incredulously.

I nod my head with no words to express how utterly depleted of everything I was by the time I got home and sat through their inquisition.

My mother shakes her head furiously. "I don't understand why you had to go out that night! We told you to stay in your room!"

"It's my fault!" My oldest sister yells, crying. "I told her she could go get pizza with her friend since you wouldn't let her go to the party."

"It's not your fault," I say to her without looking.

I can't look at anyone crying. I don't want to cry. I've never cried in front of my family since I was a baby. I'm too stubborn to show them my tears.

"You have to listen to your parents!" yells my father. "You think that we don't know anything? This is how you get yourself into trouble!"

I try to tune out, but it's impossible this time. All the yelling. I hate the yelling. I know they're upset and don't know how to deal with this, but neither do I.

"We have to hire a private investigator," says my father, refusing to let it go.

"You can't," I say. "Please, Dad. You can't. I can't live with myself if anything happens to this family because of me!" There are nearly tears in my eyes now, but I fight to keep them at bay.

"Well, you have to go to the hospital," he says.

I nod my head.

"I've had a little itch since then, down there," I say, hardly audible.

My father gets angry and says, "And you think one of *us* would know what to do? I've only been with one woman—*your mother*!"

I look over at my mother, who has her mouth open in shock. She shuts it quickly, but I don't miss that look of disbelief.

I also don't miss the implication that I'm the dirty one here in this family.

"We'll go to the hospital this weekend," he says.

I nod my head and motion to get up. No one stops me.

I go into my room and shut the door. I don't care that they can see me in one of the little monitors in the kitchen. I face the wall and let the tears flow into my pillow, trying to keep still so that they can't see me shake from the crying.

THE POWER OF HYMENS

My grandparents come over to watch the baby and kids. I'm sure they don't know what's happening, as we're not even allowed to tell them when we have the common cold. My nana worries too much when one of us gets sick, as she's lost a lot of siblings growing up in the early 1900s.

Mom, Dad, and my two older sisters take me to Children's Hospital in the city. We speak to someone about getting what they call a "rape kit"—which really bothers me because it sounds like a kit for raping.

We wait for hours to be seen. My dad is visibly upset that we have to sit in the waiting area for so long. He moans that we haven't eaten all day. It's several hours before I'm even brought in to get changed.

I half-wish I'd never told them what happened. I knew that I'd feel like a huge burden.

My mother is allowed in the room while they invade me with large metal tools. I turn my head to face the wall, trying to breathe steadily as it feels even worse than the rape itself in some ways. Maybe because I'm more present. I suddenly realize that having my mother in the room during this is deeply uncomfortable, but it's too late and too awkward to kick her out now.

Saliva is taken from my mouth and, grossly, samples are extracted from my butt. And then I'm told that all of this is probably unnecessary since I've waited too long to come in.

They give me shots and pills and an enormous needle in my ass cheek. I nearly faint. I see my father's eyes roll when I weaken, as he fears it'll only keep us longer.

"She's going to have to stay until she's stable," says a nurse.

"I'm fine," I say. She brings me some juice.

When I'm dressed and sitting back out with everyone else, one of the doctors comes forward to speak to my parents. My ears perk up.

He says, "I don't know how to say this, but it appears that everything is still intact."

I look at my father's face as his eyes well up and he says, "You mean she's still a virgin?"

The doctor sort of shrugs and tilts his head to the side. "Well, I'm just saying that the hymen isn't broken," he says, glancing over to me and then quickly back to my dad.

As we head to the garage and into the car, I'm not sure what to make of this news. What was that doctor trying to say—that I'm making everything up? I know what happened to me. Some details are fuzzy, but this much I know.

I squeezed my legs together tightly. Perhaps he didn't get all the way in? How far in does one have to get in order for it to qualify as a rape? How far is one even able to go?

We drive to the North End to the Italian restaurant we grew up going to nearly every Sunday. The owners aren't family, but we call them Aunt and Uncle. They're both fresh-off-the-boat Italians who've done well for themselves. They're good people, but I don't want to be here right now. I don't want to hide the pain and confusion behind my face but I try.

No one talks to me at dinner. They talk among themselves as if I'm not really there. I don't know what they're thinking but assume they all think that I've lied. How could I have been raped but still be a "virgin"?

I'm not a virgin! As much as I wish that I was, I can never be a virgin again. I don't want to go into all the physical details of what happened so that they'll understand.

One of the things that came up at the hospital was whether or not I'd want to go to the Rape Crisis Center. When my mom asked me in front of the nurse, I said, "No. I'll work it out on my own." Talking to a bunch of people in a room about this is the last thing that I want to do. Enough people already know as it is.

* * *

I become completely despondent in class. Eventually my teachers reach the end of their rope with me. One of them sends me down to the principal's office.

The ladies in the office smile at me and one says, "Hi Millie. What can I help you with?"

"I've been sent to see the principal," I say lowly.

A look of surprise and confusion comes over her face.

She says, "Oh... Well, follow me."

She knocks on the door, and I'm let in. I take a seat across from him on the other side of his desk, looking around the room at family photos and framed accreditations.

"This is a surprise," he says. "I can't imagine why you were sent down here."

I sit quietly until his head tilts and eyes shift, expecting a response.

"I haven't been doing my homework I guess," I say. "I've lost track of what's going on."

"I see," he says, leaning back now, casually. "If I remember correctly, you've been an honor roll student. Is everything okay at home?"

I shrug. "I guess," I say, looking out the window.

"You can talk to me," he says. "I'll keep everything in confidence."

"What if I don't want to tell you?" I say.

"Well, you don't have to," he says. "But if there's something bothering one of my honor roll students to the point of which it interferes with her work, I'd like to know."

I look him in the eye and then down at my legs. Tears flood my eyes and I say, "A few weeks ago, I was raped."

"I'm so sorry," he says. I can hear the shock and sorrow in his voice, and I can't look at him. "Was it anyone here in school?"

I shake my head and say, "No. No one from this town," still looking down.

"Does your family know?" he asks gently.

I nod and say, "Yeah. I told them last week."

"I have a daughter and can't imagine how I'd feel if this

happened to her," he tells me. "Would you mind if I tell a guidance counselor and have you speak with her about it? She's really good and can help figure out how to help you."

I don't want that. I don't want to talk to anyone else about it who will see me on a regular basis. But I say, "Yeah, okay, I guess," anyway.

I sit in a room with this older woman for a while and answer some of her questions. She says, "Do you want to go the Rape Crisis Center?"

I shrug. I don't want to, but I don't want to do anything. I don't even want to be here.

I say, "I don't know. I don't think my parents would want me to go."

My parents, like me, just want this to be over. I sure as hell don't think they want to take me back and forth to the Rape Crisis Center where everyone will know that they have a daughter who got raped. I don't even know if they believe I was raped.

"Do you mind if I speak to your parents?" she asks.

"That's fine," I say, adding, "I guess."

The call does not go over well. In fact, it goes terribly. The guidance counselor gets pushy with my mother when my mother says that I'm the one who doesn't want to go to the Rape Crisis Center.

"She doesn't know what she wants or needs right now," she says to my mother. "I strongly urge you to take her there."

I can hear my mother raising her voice through the phone, saying, "I don't care what you think! She's my daughter, and she says that she doesn't want to go!"

They hang up, and the guidance counselor huffs. She

says, "There's just no getting through to your mother," while shaking her head.

Needless to say, I dread going home. But when I do, my mother is livid. She says, "That woman has no right to tell me what I should do! Do you want to go to the Rape Crisis Center?"

I say, "No," in an attempt to keep the peace.

I've dealt with everything on my own up till now. I suppose I can deal with this too. The only problem is, music has been my greatest escape, and now it's the last thing that I want to do.

What am I going to do—perform at those same old places where Al can show up again? Maybe he'll follow me home so he can kill us all in our sleep? Or maybe, even worse, he'll bomb the house when I'm at school, killing my mother and baby brother?

Besides, I have nothing to share anymore. I've already shared too much with people I never intended to share so much with.

Music is dead to me now. It's just a part of what could have been—like me in a white lace dress. Sleazy people always swarm around musicians trying to get a piece of them anyway.

If it wasn't for my love for music, I wouldn't have wanted to be at that party next door to the recording studio so badly. I wouldn't have lied so that Roger could pick me up and lie to me, and then be lied to by Al.

Fuck music.

Fuck all of those people. I don't need their approval because none of them care about me. I don't even care about myself anymore.

Fuck virginity.

Fuck rape.

Fuck life.

If they all want to believe I'm a virgin now, I'll be a virgin if it makes them feel better. I'll play make believe again. It seems to be the only thing that I'm good at—the only way to make them happy and proud.

I'll go back to pretending to be who they want me to be. At least, then, someone will be happy instead of all of us being miserable.

I'll stop hanging around all those city kids and pop back into the white bubble. Being a misfit up here in the suburbs never made me happy, but at least it never got me raped... or *un*raped.

MAY 5, 2007 //
EXACTLY SIXTEEN YEARS
POST-INCIDENT

We're back in the basement of the Pink Haus, setting up for the party and running through the set list. I have butterflies in my stomach, but the girls are so excited. It's infectious. I try not to worry alone in my head. If they can be confident and socialize with other people, then I can too.

Nobody knows how big a deal this is for me. I haven't told Val and Terri about *The Incident* or how it made me swear off music forever sixteen years ago. They have a hint of my suicidal past, but it's never been discussed. My lyrics are often dark and that's enough. I don't need them to carry this weight alongside me.

I don't want music to have anything to do with *The Incident* anymore. I want to relaunch what music means to me. Playing music again means that I win. He doesn't get to keep that from me forever.

A couple hours before the show, the house is packed. We're wall-to-wall, room-by-room, with fellow musicians, artists, and all-around interesting people. Jackson even comes to support me, which is sweet. I don't protest to his being here. Even Max and Lacey are here despite the fact that we expected to be the band for a while.

When it's time to play, Val's new girlfriend walks around the house, ushering people on down to the basement. People are packed in so tightly that it's hard to really hone in on any one person, and I'm thankful for that. It makes it easier somehow.

I inhale and look back at Terri and Val who are taking final swigs from beer cans. Then Terri counts off with four clicks and we're doing it. We play twelve songs with people cheering and whistling in between. I won't lie. It feels kind of awesome.

It's hard to sleep at night. I keep going over our pre-show show in my head. There's just so much to think about. I can't get over how much fun playing with Val and Terri was and how it was nothing at all like it used to be sixteen years ago.

Making music with other people is so much better than playing it on my own. It doesn't have to be ugly or frightening or even a bad memory that needs escaping from. It doesn't have to be a retreat. It can just be what brings us together.

The next day we group email each other about how awesome we were. We laugh about little things that happened and share the encouraging words people said to us afterwards. We can't wait for our first big show at the club with a huge stage, professional sound system, and lighting.

The summer of 2007 is full of fun shows, dance parties, bars, and beach days. We know we're probably a little obnoxious because we're so high on life, but we don't give a shit. For various reasons, we all need this summer so badly and the friendships we build in the process.

At the end of the summer, Val makes the tough decision to put her future career ahead of the band. She's been accepted to a really good school that's six hours away. It's sad to imagine giving up the momentum we've built.

We know that we'll never have as much fun without her, but Terri and I agree to continue. We play a final show together, and I throw her a send-off party now that Jackson's moved out.

It takes a bit for us to find a third bandmate we like. Terri moves from the drums to the bass where she's more skilled and able to be in front with me. I coerce her to start singing too, and it really takes things to another level. And after many hilarious and odd auditions, we finally find a drummer who fits well with us personally and musically. We're back to booking shows in a matter of months.

Being in a band gives me a confidence that I've never had before. It's not about people telling me that I'm good or that they like what I'm doing. It's not about being in the paper, getting hit on by cute guys, or having people recognize me from a show.

It's something deeper.

I don't know—maybe it's the difference between being a dreamer and a doer. It's that feeling of action when I'm strumming the guitar, the physicality of pushing to sing over the music, and working with others on something fulfilling.

Or maybe it's something even deeper.

It's the feeling that I faced my fears head on, that I can get up on stage without worrying if it will lead to something awful. And maybe that crosses my mind in a split second here and there in my pre-show jitters. But it doesn't stop me, and that's what matters.

Or maybe it's no longer having excuses about why I can't do something—even unspoken ones tucked away in the back of my head. I'm no longer hiding behind a masked fear. I feel empowered.

Millie 1, Rapist 0.

FORGIVENESS

I share with my homeopath how it feels to reclaim music with my new band. She's impressed with how quickly my energy is shifting. I am too, but I don't want to slow down to think about it too much. I just want to be living in the present—which she says is exactly where she wants me to be. It's a sign of health, she says.

Excitedly, I also divulge what having my newfound Lily family is doing for me. Speaking to someone—to her—out loud about it, unlocks another answer to a nagging question I've always had.

Why did I want to kill myself at such a young age? Why was I filled with so much pain as a child when I should've just looked on the bright side, feeling lucky and grateful?

Because, despite how my adoption story read from the outside, I was more than just a child from a third-world country who was rescued and given a loving home. That was one side of the story. I was also an infant separated

from her mother. During one of the most critical times of
my life, I didn't feel safe or nurtured. I was in an unstable
and ever-changing environment—from my birth mother to
an adoption agency to an orphanage to a foster mother and
then eventually to a family who looked nothing like anyone
I'd seen and spoke a language I'd never heard.

I was raised among children who all looked and spoke
very much like my new parents, which emphasized my dif-
ferences with each new sibling born, no matter how much
they might have wanted to believe that I was one of them.
And my conflicting feelings of not being like them only
made me feel guilty for not feeling as lucky as everyone else
thought that I should be.

I don't believe that I ever wanted to die, but as a young
child, I had no way to channel my feelings without worrying
about hurting anyone else. I knew that my feelings were my
problems, as nobody else seemed to believe I should have
any. And so dying felt like the only escape from living as an
imposter in my very own skin.

Of course, once my mother found my diary that day, I
saw how upset my true feelings made her. I knew then that
I had to carry on hiding and living for her because I couldn't
bear to make her that unhappy again.

I was doing okay until *The Incident* happened. Things
just got compounded. I believe a part of me hated my
mother for making me feel like I had to continue to live on
through my own misery.

One day, in the bathtub in Key West, I remember sitting
there on the edge as I did with the knife, shaking and exert-
ing fluids from my face. I wrote in my notebook, *"I'm sorry,
Mom,"* and exploded into another fit of tears. I didn't un-

derstand that until now. I wanted her to know that, if I managed to do it that time, that I was sorry for breaking my promise I made at age seven. I'd have let her down.

As my homeopath said, in order to heal effectively, you start with your most current pains and move backwards. When you get down to the original pain, you are truly freed to lift yourself up and out.

I have many complications with my mother, even still, but I love her unconditionally—even when loving her hurts me because she can't give me what I need, which is mostly time. And as much as I love my mother and have lived for her sake until now, I've decided that it's time to start living for my own sake. I need to build a life that feels honest to my needs and what will make *me* proud to be alive.

Looking back, I don't feel that tearing up pages of my diary and flushing them down the toilet was the right thing to do. But I do believe it's the best she was capable of at the time with so much else going on.

I don't believe that guilting someone—a child—into living is good, yet I'm thankful it has gotten me to this point. We can't go back and rewrite the past, so I must move forward with the knowledge and strength that I've gained along the way.

I don't even believe that I should have to feel grateful for being adopted because the truth is, nobody knows what else life might have been for me. We don't know if my first mother died, what she'd been through, or what might have led her to feel that relinquishing me was for the best. We don't know what my life could have been, had Korea accepted and supported unwed mothers. That said, I'm not ungrateful for the good memories I've made with my adoptive family, nor what we've done for each other. Oftentimes I still feel like an outsider and a misfit, but I love them all.

I don't accept the concept that everything happens for a reason but that sometimes you can make something good in the aftermath of horror.

Through this journey, I am learning that people don't have to feel grateful for what has led them to where they are. They just have to make peace with it and find something within themselves that gives them the will to move on.

I'm alive. I've made it here, and the rest of my life is all mine. I can do anything I want with it. Just acknowledging that is so freeing.

Abandonment issues that I have resulting from my debut into this life may always be a struggle, and I accept that. I realize how deep they run through me and how far back it goes. But it is what it is, I suppose. There's nothing I can do to resolve things, short of cultivating healthy relationships over time.

I initiated a birth family search and was told that, being abandoned without a note, that kind of closure is unlikely. Part of me is saddened, yet part of me is relieved. Perhaps it's selfishness, but after all I've been through, I don't know if I want to welcome another family into my life. I'd have to learn Korean and invest in even more people's emotions and perspectives. It's daunting and overwhelming—but maybe someday I won't feel this way.

Right now, I'm ready to start living my life for me. I believe I have earned it.

LIAM

I've been dating an older, well-respected local musician for several months. I resisted him for a while but began to find him exciting and endearing. We go to shows and parties together and have fun overindulging. But it's not love.

I took the opportunity to explore beyond my comfort zone. I even dated a girl for a little while. She was smart, successful, beautiful, and pretty badass. But as it turns out, that dynamic doesn't work well for me either. Or maybe it's just that we weren't aligned.

I start to fear that I'm too smart and too bitter to ever fall in love again—or perhaps for the first time. I think maybe I've experienced too much heartache already. I convince myself that it's okay, not everybody needs to fall in love. There are other ways to live a fulfilling life alone.

One cold winter night, I just want to go dance somewhere to get out of my head. I find out that some friends will be at this club for an eighties alternative dance night called "Heroes."

I get dressed and call a cab. I'm no longer afraid to show up at places alone. I always know I'll run into some people I've met or want to meet. And sure enough, I walk in to tons of people I know and am happy to see. I grab a drink and hit the floor.

The music is perfect. I dance in small groups and move along to chat with others. Then I see this guy moving through the crowd. I've never seen him before but am struck by his presence somehow. It's as if the music fades into the background, and there's a light shining down onto him.

I maneuver across the floor between people spilling drinks on my clothes and my feet and couldn't be any less concerned. I stand next to the girls that I came here to meet. And as introductions are being made, I squeeze myself into the mix.

His name is Liam, and I trail him to the bar like a stalker. I find out he's from Ireland.

"Do you have a green card?" I ask, because, well, I feel I have to after what I went through with Seamus.

"My family and I became citizens a while back," he says.

"Oh," I say, relieved. "Where in Ireland are you from?"

"Cork and Dublin," he says.

"I lived in Dublin for a while," I say. "I lived in Galway for a couple years too. Where in Dublin did you live?"

"You wouldn't know it," he says. "It's a town called Ranelagh."

"I do know it," I smile. "I lived in Rathmines, just a few hundred feet from Ranelagh."

"No way," he says, surprised. "I lived right on the border

of Rathmines."

We spend the night dancing and making bets on who would win in a game of Boggle. No longer needing to try to be cool, I embrace my dorkiness.

"I'm afraid I'm the reigning Boggle Queen," I tell him. "You might want to forfeit to save your ego in advance."

"We'll see about that," he teases.

I excitedly tell Terri all about this guy Liam. I fall to the floor laughing in band practice over what's likely nothing. I'm giddy since the night we met. Everything is hysterical somehow.

The following week, I find myself lounging around in a tank top he left at my place. In my underwear and his shirt, I write the most embarrassing puppy love song I've ever written. I decide to send it to him only to freak out hours later, wishing I could retract. But since I sent him an actual file rather than a link, I'm shit out of luck. It's hours before he's home from work and able to respond.

"I liked your song," he says, finally. "It kind of reminds me of Mazzy Star."

I exhale. *Relief.*

Liam is a musician as well. He's in a couple of different bands. We spend hours lying around together, playing music, and talking nonsense. He's also a naturally talented artist. We draw portraits of each other sometimes.

As if all of that weren't enough, he's also a vegetarian— like me—so it makes cooking dinner together fairly easy, despite his bossiness in the kitchen.

When I'm not around him, I feel more balanced than I have in past relationship beginnings. However, now and then when I indulge it, I become desperately afraid that he's not going to stay. Secure in the great things I've got going on, old insecurities are still hard to break. So I lie around in bed one day taking suggestive photos. I send him one.

I typically hear back from Liam within hours of sending a text. Understanding his workday schedule, I try not to freak out during the wait, but I do.

What are you up to? I text again, later that evening.

Just thinking about dinner, he texts.

Want to come make some together? I reply.

He comes around about an hour later. I beam at him ear-to-ear through the window before opening the door. While we're chopping vegetables I say, "So did you get the pic I sent earlier?"

There's a pause, and he says, "Yeah," but nothing more.

"What did you think?" I ask, feeling awkward and extremely vulnerable.

There's another pause and he says, "I liked it, but when I got it I was thinking, 'She doesn't have to do that.'"

Past lovers would practically beg for suggestive—not to be mistaken for pornographic—photos. It was something I comfortably accepted as a man's desire, which I was happy to fulfill if it meant keeping him interested. However, this type of behavior actually put Liam off.

For once, I find myself in a relationship with someone who doesn't need or want me to objectify myself for him. I have to say that it leaves me bewildered. I'm questioning everything I thought I knew about how to keep a man happy. From here on, I vow to approach things differently, and it seems to be working.

On March 19—my second known Found Day—I book the band a show with the hottest local club in the area. It's a night called "The Pill" that plays Brit pop dance music, featuring one band in between DJ sets. There's a built-in crowd comprised of many new acquaintances. The night sells out.

We set up balloons and plan a couple of surprise confetti bombs toward the end of our set. I've never felt such a natural buzz on stage as I do this night. I peer over toward Terri periodically and see that she's feeling it too. Looking out to the crowd through colorful strands of confetti, I smile widely as I play my heart out.

The next morning in bed, Liam looks at me and says, "Millie, where on God's green earth did you come from?"

"I have no idea," I say to him, shaking my head. "All I know is I was found in Korea."

He smirks and I giggle, suddenly aware of rhetorics.

My heart swoons, as I can hardly believe my life. I'm recording my first album with the band and living in a great apartment on my own; I have a new novel out to prospective agents, and I'm in bed with this beautiful man.

I'm almost afraid to think it, but then I say fuck it.

This might be love.

EPILOGUE

Given the provocative nature of this book and how it exposes my dark past, I've struggled with whether or not to write it quite a bit. Some chapters were excruciating. At times, I nearly quit. I grappled with whether it was worth the emotional toll it would take on me—and perhaps others who shared these parts of my life. I considered whether it would be helpful to anyone at all and if it was healthy for me to dredge through the past so deeply. After all, I have worked so hard to create a happy present. I wanted to focus on the good of the now and forget about where I've been.

However, without telling and sharing this story, I felt like I was continuing life as an imposter—only showing the best of who I am now. It also felt increasingly selfish not to complete it. Knowing how alone and ashamed I have felt in the past, I wanted to help encourage dialogue about what a trauma such as rape can have on a life.

I believe there are reasons why we've all done what

we've done, and we don't need to hide our experiences from ourselves or others anymore. Talking about the ugly parts of our lives is not always focusing on the negative. I believe that sometimes, in order to move on internally, we need to fully embrace the things we're not proud of before we can truly release them. And by doing so, we can help empower others.

I have learned so much by forcing myself through this process of writing. I have cried to and cringed at myself. But, mostly, I have gained a much greater love and respect for myself and the ones who shared time with me.

We are all flawed. We are all human. We don't always make the right choices, and that's okay most of the time. I think that what really matters is usually what follows.

I've dug deep into the pit of my soul and made myself vulnerable to the world. I expect criticism will follow. However, if my story helps one person to feel less alone, helps people push through their own difficulties, shame, and learn to live for and accept themselves, then I'm good with the rest.

The best thing about making it out the other side is knowing how resilient you are.

* * *

I chose to change names, minor details, and sequencing due to privacy and brevity. While I'm sure the story varies in parts from others' perspectives, it is written from my own personal memory, perspective, and truth.

ACKNOWLEDGEMENTS

I'd like to thank the following people for taking a leap of faith to blindly support and encourage this gritty project: Abby Heredia, Anders Nielsen, Angela Aspers, Anne Lehman, Anonymous, Anonymous 2, Becky Kay, Becky Tanger, Brendan Clarke, Bruce Kohl, Bryn Bennett, Carrie Holmes, Claudia Rocha, Debbi Wagner-Johnson, Dennis White, Diane Shigley, Grace Pittman, Hugh Wyman, Jen Kim, Jessica Molinaro, John Robinson, Kacie Rater, Kat Park, Kelly Savage, Kevin Lin, Mary Mui, Mary Flatley, Michael J. Epstein, Mindy Greenville, Nicole Henriksen, Pam van der Feest, Rachel and Bo Barringer, Rebecca Bourdeau, Richard Monti, Rick Pinchera, Ron Rhodes, Ryan Clark, Shanna K. Ferber, Susan Major, Susannah Buzard, Tanya Kaanta, Val Russell, and Yelarney Hibberd.

To Erika Fisher—for providing detailed and thoughtful editorial guidance and encouragement.

To Cynthia Chrisman—my patient, empathetic, and

highly skilled therapist/homeopath, for working with me through my years in need and getting me to a place in which I don't need her care any longer.

To my husband and most favorite person—for being himself and allowing me to fully be myself, offering sup-port in many ways without hesitation or concern about this book.

To my family—for never asking me not to write this book, despite unspoken fears and privacy concerns.

To my exes—those I am friends with and those I am not—for walking alongside me for a while and allowing me to grow.

To my Lily family—for their daily presence, friendship, willingness to share, connect, heal, and grow with me.

To *Land of Gazillion Adoptees*, *Seoul Searching*, Jane Jeong Trenka, and everybody who commits their life's work toward giving transracial adoptees a voice, lobbying for change, and creating awareness.

To all the women and men who are brave enough to speak out against rape culture, expose the truth, and work toward change.

And, finally, to my Nana—for being there for me and loving me, even when I was likely unlovable by most.

Please review this book online.
It will increase visibility for others to find it,
and help those who are considering buying this book
decide if it's right for them.

http://itwasntlove.com/reviews

For more information on this book—
including special features and ways to connect
with myself and other readers:

http://itwasntlove.com

Made in the USA
San Bernardino, CA
24 October 2014